College Visit Journal

- Erik Kopp, BE, MBA

This book provides a handy journal to take along on your college visits to enable you to quickly and easily keep track of all the information you learn and need to know in a single place using a consistent format, and you won't forget to ask any questions. This way you can more easily compare all your college visit experiences and use this information to help guide you and your family in your search for the right college for you.

Published By:

EK Publications
www.ekpublications.com
ekpublications@gmail.com

Name of College Visited	Page
College 1:	3
College 2:	9
College 3:	15
College 4:	21
College 5:	27
College 6:	33
College 7:	39
College 8:	45
College 9:	51
College 10:	57
College 11:	63
College 12:	69
College 13:	75
College 14:	81
College 15:	87
College 16:	93
College 17:	99
College 18:	105
College 19:	111
College 20:	117
College 21:	123
College 22:	129
College 23:	135
College 24:	141
College 25:	147

BEFORE YOU GO (Page 1 of 6)

Name of College:____

Location (Street Address):____

Website URL:______________________________ Phone #:______________________________

Type of Visit: ☐ Online (Virtual) / ☐ On Site (Tour) Date of Planned On Site Visit:____________

Size of College: ☐ Small (less than 5,000 students) / ☐ Medium (5,000 to 15,000 students) /
☐ Large (more than 15,000 students)

Type of College: ☐ Liberal Arts / ☐ Science & Engineering / ☐ General Studies
☐ College (Undergraduate only) / ☐ University (Undergraduate & Graduate)
☐ State/Community College / ☐ Private College
☐ 2 Year Undergraduate / ☐ 4 Year Undergraduate

Dates / Times of Tours and Information Sessions:____

Do I know people who are / will be attending this college? ☐ No / ☐ Yes – Name(s):______________

____

Do I know people who have graduated from this college? ☐ No / ☐ Yes – Name(s):______________

____

I am interested in this college because:____

____

Things I have heard about this college are:____

____

WHEN YOU GET THERE (Page 2 of 6)

Name of College:____

Date of Visit:________________________ Time of Visit:________________________

Was school in session when I visited: ☐ Yes / ☐ No

Activities during On Site Visit (check all that apply):

☐ Campus Tour / ☐ Information Session / ☐ Interview / ☐ Tour of Surrounding Area

Surrounding Area: ☐ Rural (Country) / ☐ Suburban (Near residential area) / ☐ Urban (City)

Names of people who presented / people I met with and contact information (phone, email).

____

____

____

Topics discussed at Information Session / notes (see next page for list of possible questions to ask):

____

____

____

____

____

____

____

____

____

____

____

____

WHILE YOU ARE THERE (Page 3 of 6)

Name of College:______________________________

Questions you can ask (some ideas – feel free to modify these or add more):

- What are entrance requirements (GPA, SAT, SAT2, ACT, AP courses, Honors Courses)? ______________________________
- What is the graduation rate (% of incoming freshmen who will graduate)? ________________
- What percent of classes are taught by professors vs. teaching assistants? ________________
- What is the average class size (Student : Teacher ratio)? ____________________
- What is the expected size of the freshman class? ________________________
- When is the application deadline (regular and early decision)? ______________________________
- When do I need to declare my major and how easy is it to change? ________________
- Do I need to write a thesis to graduate? ________________________
- Do you take transfer credits? ____________________________
- What learning opportunities are there outside of the classroom (i.e. internships, coop, research programs)? ______________________________
- How many students typically study abroad? ________________________
- Are there fraternities and sororities, and what percent of the students belong to one? ________
- What are the popular extracurricular activities? ________________________
- Is there employment placement assistance for graduating seniors? ________________
- What is the cost for tuition? Room and Board? Books and supplies? ________________
- Is there Financial Aid and/or Scholarships available? How do I apply? ________________
- Can freshman live off campus? Can they have a car on campus? ________________
- Do most students stay on campus over weekends or leave? ____________________
- Other questions I have: ____________________________
- NOTES:

____

____

____

____

____

____

WHAT I LEARNED ABOUT THIS COLLEGE (Page 4 of 6)

Name of College:____

Majors Offered:____

Places I visited during my tour and what I thought of them
Check all that apply and rank from 1 [bad] to 5 [excellent]:

☐ Student Center (-1 2 3 4 5+) comment:____________________________

☐ Computer Center (-1 2 3 4 5+) comment:____________________________

☐ Labs (-1 2 3 4 5+) comment:___________________________________

☐ Lecture Halls (-1 2 3 4 5+) comment:_____________________________

☐ Classrooms (-1 2 3 4 5+) comment:_______________________________

☐ Department Bldg for my major (-1 2 3 4 5+) comment:___________________

☐ Dormitories (-1 2 3 4 5+) comment:_______________________________

☐ Athletic Center / Gym (-1 2 3 4 5+) comment:_________________________

☐ Library (-1 2 3 4 5+) comment:_________________________________

☐ School Store (-1 2 3 4 5+) comment:______________________________

☐ Dining Hall (-1 2 3 4 5+) comment:_______________________________

☐ Other__________________ (-1 2 3 4 5+) comment:___________________

☐ Other__________________ (-1 2 3 4 5+) comment:___________________

☐ Other__________________ (-1 2 3 4 5+) comment:___________________

How was the food?____

What did I think about the campus and the surrounding area:_____________________

____

What did I think about the students and the staff I met? Would I fit in well here? ____________

____

What did I think about the courses of study offered here? Do these meet my goals?__________

____

What did I think about the extracurricular activities offered here? ______________________

OVERALL ASSESSMENT and FOLLOW UP ACTIONS (Page 5 of 6)

Name of College:______________________________

What I like best about this college is:______________________________

____

____

____

What I like least about this college is:______________________________

____

____

____

Follow up actions / next steps I need to do are:______________________________

____

____

____

My overall assessment: (-1 2 3 4 5+) comment:______________________________

My Parents' overall assessment: (-1 2 3 4 5+) comment:______________________________

Additional Notes:

____

____

____

____

____

____

____

____

____

____

____

____

Name of College:____

Page 6 of 6 - STAPLE / ATTACH ANY HANDOUTS, MAPS, ETC HERE:

— —

BEFORE YOU GO (Page 1 of 6)

Name of College:____

Location (Street Address):____________________________________

Website URL:____________________ Phone #:____________________

Type of Visit: ☐ Online (Virtual) / ☐ On Site (Tour) Date of Planned On Site Visit:__________

Size of College: ☐ Small (less than 5,000 students) / ☐ Medium (5,000 to 15,000 students) /
☐ Large (more than 15,000 students)

Type of College: ☐ Liberal Arts / ☐ Science & Engineering / ☐ General Studies
☐ College (Undergraduate only) / ☐ University (Undergraduate & Graduate)
☐ State/Community College / ☐ Private College
☐ 2 Year Undergraduate / ☐ 4 Year Undergraduate

Dates / Times of Tours and Information Sessions:____________________________________

Do I know people who are / will be attending this college? ☐ No / ☐ Yes – Name(s):__________

____

Do I know people who have graduated from this college? ☐ No / ☐ Yes – Name(s):__________

____

I am interested in this college because:______________________________

____

Things I have heard about this college are:____________________________

____

WHEN YOU GET THERE (Page 2 of 6)

Name of College:____

Date of Visit:_______________________ Time of Visit:_______________________

Was school in session when I visited: ☐ Yes / ☐ No

Activities during On Site Visit (check all that apply):

☐ Campus Tour / ☐ Information Session / ☐ Interview / ☐ Tour of Surrounding Area

Surrounding Area: ☐ Rural (Country) / ☐ Suburban (Near residential area) / ☐ Urban (City)

Names of people who presented / people I met with and contact information (phone, email).

Topics discussed at Information Session / notes (see next page for list of possible questions to ask):

WHILE YOU ARE THERE (Page 3 of 6)

Name of College:____________________________________

Questions you can ask (some ideas – feel free to modify these or add more):

- What are entrance requirements (GPA, SAT, SAT2, ACT, AP courses, Honors Courses)? ____________________
- What is the graduation rate (% of incoming freshmen who will graduate)? __________
- What percent of classes are taught by professors vs. teaching assistants? __________
- What is the average class size (Student : Teacher ratio)? __________
- What is the expected size of the freshman class? __________
- When is the application deadline (regular and early decision)? ____________________
- When do I need to declare my major and how easy is it to change? __________
- Do I need to write a thesis to graduate? __________
- Do you take transfer credits? __________
- What learning opportunities are there outside of the classroom (i.e. internships, coop, research programs)? __________
- How many students typically study abroad? __________
- Are there fraternities and sororities, and what percent of the students belong to one? __________
- What are the popular extracurricular activities? __________
- Is there employment placement assistance for graduating seniors? __________
- What is the cost for tuition? Room and Board? Books and supplies? __________
- Is there Financial Aid and/or Scholarships available? How do I apply? __________
- Can freshman live off campus? Can they have a car on campus? __________
- Do most students stay on campus over weekends or leave? __________
- Other questions I have: __________
- NOTES:

____

____

____

____

____

____

WHAT I LEARNED ABOUT THIS COLLEGE (Page 4 of 6)

Name of College:____

Majors Offered:____

Places I visited during my tour and what I thought of them
Check all that apply and rank from 1 [bad] to 5 [excellent]:

☐ Student Center (-1 2 3 4 5+) comment:______________________

☐ Computer Center (-1 2 3 4 5+) comment:______________________

☐ Labs (-1 2 3 4 5+) comment:______________________

☐ Lecture Halls (-1 2 3 4 5+) comment:______________________

☐ Classrooms (-1 2 3 4 5+) comment:______________________

☐ Department Bldg for my major (-1 2 3 4 5+) comment:______________________

☐ Dormitories (-1 2 3 4 5+) comment:______________________

☐ Athletic Center / Gym (-1 2 3 4 5+) comment:______________________

☐ Library (-1 2 3 4 5+) comment:______________________

☐ School Store (-1 2 3 4 5+) comment:______________________

☐ Dining Hall (-1 2 3 4 5+) comment:______________________

☐ Other__________________ (-1 2 3 4 5+) comment:______________________

☐ Other__________________ (-1 2 3 4 5+) comment:______________________

☐ Other__________________ (-1 2 3 4 5+) comment:______________________

How was the food?____

What did I think about the campus and the surrounding area:______________________

____

What did I think about the students and the staff I met? Would I fit in well here? ______________

____

What did I think about the courses of study offered here? Do these meet my goals?______________

____

What did I think about the extracurricular activities offered here? ______________________

OVERALL ASSESSMENT and FOLLOW UP ACTIONS (Page 5 of 6)

Name of College:____________________________________

What I like best about this college is:____________________________

What I like least about this college is:____________________________

Follow up actions / next steps I need to do are:________________________

My overall assessment: (-1 2 3 4 5+) comment:__________________

My Parents' overall assessment: (-1 2 3 4 5+) comment:______________

Additional Notes:

Name of College:____

Page 6 of 6 - STAPLE / ATTACH ANY HANDOUTS, MAPS, ETC HERE:

— —

BEFORE YOU GO (Page 1 of 6)

Name of College:____

Location (Street Address):____

Website URL:______________________________ Phone #:_____________________________

Type of Visit: ☐ Online (Virtual) / ☐ On Site (Tour) Date of Planned On Site Visit:____________

Size of College: ☐ Small (less than 5,000 students) / ☐ Medium (5,000 to 15,000 students) /

☐ Large (more than 15,000 students)

Type of College: ☐ Liberal Arts / ☐ Science & Engineering / ☐ General Studies

☐ College (Undergraduate only) / ☐ University (Undergraduate & Graduate)

☐ State/Community College / ☐ Private College

☐ 2 Year Undergraduate / ☐ 4 Year Undergraduate

Dates / Times of Tours and Information
Sessions:____

Do I know people who are / will be attending this college? ☐ No / ☐ Yes – Name(s):_____________

____

Do I know people who have graduated from this college? ☐ No / ☐ Yes – Name(s):______________

____

I am interested in this college because:____

____

Things I have heard about this college are:____

____

WHEN YOU GET THERE (Page 2 of 6)

Name of College:____

Date of Visit:__________________________ Time of Visit:__________________________

Was school in session when I visited: ☐ Yes / ☐ No

Activities during On Site Visit (check all that apply):

☐ Campus Tour / ☐ Information Session / ☐ Interview / ☐ Tour of Surrounding Area

Surrounding Area: ☐ Rural (Country) / ☐ Suburban (Near residential area) / ☐ Urban (City)

Names of people who presented / people I met with and contact information (phone, email).

____

____

____

Topics discussed at Information Session / notes (see next page for list of possible questions to ask):

____

____

____

____

____

____

____

____

____

____

____

____

WHILE YOU ARE THERE (Page 3 of 6)

Name of College:____

Questions you can ask (some ideas – feel free to modify these or add more):

- What are entrance requirements (GPA, SAT, SAT2, ACT, AP courses, Honors Courses)? ____
- What is the graduation rate (% of incoming freshmen who will graduate)? ________________
- What percent of classes are taught by professors vs. teaching assistants? ________________
- What is the average class size (Student : Teacher ratio)? __________________________
- What is the expected size of the freshman class? _______________________________
- When is the application deadline (regular and early decision)? ____
- When do I need to declare my major and how easy is it to change? ____________________
- Do I need to write a thesis to graduate? _____________________________________
- Do you take transfer credits? ____
- What learning opportunities are there outside of the classroom (i.e. internships, coop, research programs)? ____
- How many students typically study abroad? ___________________________________
- Are there fraternities and sororities, and what percent of the students belong to one? ________
- What are the popular extracurricular activities? ________________________________
- Is there employment placement assistance for graduating seniors? ____________________
- What is the cost for tuition? Room and Board? Books and supplies? __________________
- Is there Financial Aid and/or Scholarships available? How do I apply? _________________
- Can freshman live off campus? Can they have a car on campus? _____________________
- Do most students stay on campus over weekends or leave? _________________________
- Other questions I have: ____
- NOTES:

____

____

____

____

____

____

WHAT I LEARNED ABOUT THIS COLLEGE (Page 4 of 6)

Name of College:____

Majors Offered:____

Places I visited during my tour and what I thought of them
Check all that apply and rank from 1 [bad] to 5 [excellent]:

☐ Student Center (-1 2 3 4 5+) comment:____________________

☐ Computer Center (-1 2 3 4 5+) comment:____________________

☐ Labs (-1 2 3 4 5+) comment:____________________

☐ Lecture Halls (-1 2 3 4 5+) comment:____________________

☐ Classrooms (-1 2 3 4 5+) comment:____________________

☐ Department Bldg for my major (-1 2 3 4 5+) comment:____________________

☐ Dormitories (-1 2 3 4 5+) comment:____________________

☐ Athletic Center / Gym (-1 2 3 4 5+) comment:____________________

☐ Library (-1 2 3 4 5+) comment:____________________

☐ School Store (-1 2 3 4 5+) comment:____________________

☐ Dining Hall (-1 2 3 4 5+) comment:____________________

☐ Other____________________ (-1 2 3 4 5+) comment:____________________

☐ Other____________________ (-1 2 3 4 5+) comment:____________________

☐ Other____________________ (-1 2 3 4 5+) comment:____________________

How was the food?____

What did I think about the campus and the surrounding area:____________________

____

What did I think about the students and the staff I met? Would I fit in well here? ____________________

____

What did I think about the courses of study offered here? Do these meet my goals?____________________

____

What did I think about the extracurricular activities offered here? ____________________

OVERALL ASSESSMENT and FOLLOW UP ACTIONS (Page 5 of 6)

Name of College:____

What I like best about this college is:____

____

____

____

What I like least about this college is:____

____

____

____

Follow up actions / next steps I need to do are:____

____

____

____

My overall assessment: (-1 2 3 4 5+) comment:____________________

My Parents' overall assessment: (-1 2 3 4 5+) comment:____________________

Additional Notes:

____

____

____

____

____

____

____

____

____

____

____

____

Name of College:____

Page 6 of 6 - STAPLE / ATTACH ANY HANDOUTS, MAPS, ETC HERE:

— —

BEFORE YOU GO (Page 1 of 6)

Name of College:____

Location (Street Address):____________________________________

Website URL:____________________ Phone #:____________________

Type of Visit: ☐ Online (Virtual) / ☐ On Site (Tour) Date of Planned On Site Visit:__________

Size of College: ☐ Small (less than 5,000 students) / ☐ Medium (5,000 to 15,000 students) /
☐ Large (more than 15,000 students)

Type of College: ☐ Liberal Arts / ☐ Science & Engineering / ☐ General Studies
☐ College (Undergraduate only) / ☐ University (Undergraduate & Graduate)
☐ State/Community College / ☐ Private College
☐ 2 Year Undergraduate / ☐ 4 Year Undergraduate

Dates / Times of Tours and Information Sessions:____________________________________

Do I know people who are / will be attending this college? ☐ No / ☐ Yes – Name(s):__________

____

Do I know people who have graduated from this college? ☐ No / ☐ Yes – Name(s):__________

____

I am interested in this college because:________________________________

____

Things I have heard about this college are:______________________________

____

WHEN YOU GET THERE (Page 2 of 6)

Name of College:____

Date of Visit:____________________________ Time of Visit:____________________________

Was school in session when I visited: ☐ Yes / ☐ No

Activities during On Site Visit (check all that apply):

☐ Campus Tour / ☐ Information Session / ☐ Interview / ☐ Tour of Surrounding Area

Surrounding Area: ☐ Rural (Country) / ☐ Suburban (Near residential area) / ☐ Urban (City)

Names of people who presented / people I met with and contact information (phone, email).

____

____

____

Topics discussed at Information Session / notes (see next page for list of possible questions to ask):

____

____

____

____

____

____

____

____

____

____

____

____

WHILE YOU ARE THERE (Page 3 of 6)

Name of College: ____________________

Questions you can ask (some ideas – feel free to modify these or add more):

- What are entrance requirements (GPA, SAT, SAT2, ACT, AP courses, Honors Courses)? ____________________
- What is the graduation rate (% of incoming freshmen who will graduate)? ____________________
- What percent of classes are taught by professors vs. teaching assistants? ____________________
- What is the average class size (Student : Teacher ratio)? ____________________
- What is the expected size of the freshman class? ____________________
- When is the application deadline (regular and early decision)? ____________________
- When do I need to declare my major and how easy is it to change? ____________________
- Do I need to write a thesis to graduate? ____________________
- Do you take transfer credits? ____________________
- What learning opportunities are there outside of the classroom (i.e. internships, coop, research programs)? ____________________
- How many students typically study abroad? ____________________
- Are there fraternities and sororities, and what percent of the students belong to one? ____________________
- What are the popular extracurricular activities? ____________________
- Is there employment placement assistance for graduating seniors? ____________________
- What is the cost for tuition? Room and Board? Books and supplies? ____________________
- Is there Financial Aid and/or Scholarships available? How do I apply? ____________________
- Can freshman live off campus? Can they have a car on campus? ____________________
- Do most students stay on campus over weekends or leave? ____________________
- Other questions I have: ____________________
- NOTES:

____

____

____

____

____

____

WHAT I LEARNED ABOUT THIS COLLEGE (Page 4 of 6)

Name of College:____

Majors Offered:____

Places I visited during my tour and what I thought of them
Check all that apply and rank from 1 [bad] to 5 [excellent]:

☐ Student Center (-1 2 3 4 5+) comment:________________________

☐ Computer Center (-1 2 3 4 5+) comment:________________________

☐ Labs (-1 2 3 4 5+) comment:________________________

☐ Lecture Halls (-1 2 3 4 5+) comment:________________________

☐ Classrooms (-1 2 3 4 5+) comment:________________________

☐ Department Bldg for my major (-1 2 3 4 5+) comment:________________________

☐ Dormitories (-1 2 3 4 5+) comment:________________________

☐ Athletic Center / Gym (-1 2 3 4 5+) comment:________________________

☐ Library (-1 2 3 4 5+) comment:________________________

☐ School Store (-1 2 3 4 5+) comment:________________________

☐ Dining Hall (-1 2 3 4 5+) comment:________________________

☐ Other________________ (-1 2 3 4 5+) comment:________________________

☐ Other________________ (-1 2 3 4 5+) comment:________________________

☐ Other________________ (-1 2 3 4 5+) comment:________________________

How was the food?____

What did I think about the campus and the surrounding area:________________________

____

What did I think about the students and the staff I met? Would I fit in well here? ________________

____

What did I think about the courses of study offered here? Do these meet my goals?________________

____

What did I think about the extracurricular activities offered here? ________________________

OVERALL ASSESSMENT and FOLLOW UP ACTIONS (Page 5 of 6)

Name of College:____

What I like best about this college is:______________________________

What I like least about this college is:______________________________

Follow up actions / next steps I need to do are:__________________________

My overall assessment: (-1 2 3 4 5+) comment:______________________

My Parents' overall assessment: (-1 2 3 4 5+) comment:__________________

Additional Notes:

Name of College:____

Page 6 of 6 - STAPLE / ATTACH ANY HANDOUTS, MAPS, ETC HERE:

— —

BEFORE YOU GO (Page 1 of 6)

Name of College:____

Location (Street Address):____

Website URL:________________________ Phone #:________________________

Type of Visit: ☐ Online (Virtual) / ☐ On Site (Tour) Date of Planned On Site Visit:____________

Size of College: ☐ Small (less than 5,000 students) / ☐ Medium (5,000 to 15,000 students) /

☐ Large (more than 15,000 students)

Type of College: ☐ Liberal Arts / ☐ Science & Engineering / ☐ General Studies

☐ College (Undergraduate only) / ☐ University (Undergraduate & Graduate)

☐ State/Community College / ☐ Private College

☐ 2 Year Undergraduate / ☐ 4 Year Undergraduate

Dates / Times of Tours and Information
Sessions:____

Do I know people who are / will be attending this college? ☐ No / ☐ Yes – Name(s):____________

____

Do I know people who have graduated from this college? ☐ No / ☐ Yes – Name(s):____________

____

I am interested in this college because:________________________________

____

Things I have heard about this college are:______________________________

____

WHEN YOU GET THERE (Page 2 of 6)

Name of College:____

Date of Visit:____________________ Time of Visit:____________________

Was school in session when I visited: ☐ Yes / ☐ No

Activities during On Site Visit (check all that apply):

☐ Campus Tour / ☐ Information Session / ☐ Interview / ☐ Tour of Surrounding Area

Surrounding Area: ☐ Rural (Country) / ☐ Suburban (Near residential area) / ☐ Urban (City)

Names of people who presented / people I met with and contact information (phone, email).

Topics discussed at Information Session / notes (see next page for list of possible questions to ask):

WHILE YOU ARE THERE (Page 3 of 6)

Name of College:____

Questions you can ask (some ideas – feel free to modify these or add more):

- What are entrance requirements (GPA, SAT, SAT2, ACT, AP courses, Honors Courses)? ________________________
- What is the graduation rate (% of incoming freshmen who will graduate)? __________
- What percent of classes are taught by professors vs. teaching assistants? __________
- What is the average class size (Student : Teacher ratio)? __________
- What is the expected size of the freshman class? __________
- When is the application deadline (regular and early decision)? ________________________
- When do I need to declare my major and how easy is it to change? __________
- Do I need to write a thesis to graduate? __________
- Do you take transfer credits? __________
- What learning opportunities are there outside of the classroom (i.e. internships, coop, research programs)? __________
- How many students typically study abroad? __________
- Are there fraternities and sororities, and what percent of the students belong to one? __________
- What are the popular extracurricular activities? __________
- Is there employment placement assistance for graduating seniors? __________
- What is the cost for tuition? Room and Board? Books and supplies? __________
- Is there Financial Aid and/or Scholarships available? How do I apply? __________
- Can freshman live off campus? Can they have a car on campus? __________
- Do most students stay on campus over weekends or leave? __________
- Other questions I have: __________
- NOTES:

____

____

____

____

____

____

WHAT I LEARNED ABOUT THIS COLLEGE (Page 4 of 6)

Name of College:____

Majors Offered:____

Places I visited during my tour and what I thought of them
Check all that apply and rank from 1 [bad] to 5 [excellent]:

☐ Student Center (-1 2 3 4 5+) comment:________________________

☐ Computer Center (-1 2 3 4 5+) comment:________________________

☐ Labs (-1 2 3 4 5+) comment:________________________

☐ Lecture Halls (-1 2 3 4 5+) comment:________________________

☐ Classrooms (-1 2 3 4 5+) comment:________________________

☐ Department Bldg for my major (-1 2 3 4 5+) comment:________________________

☐ Dormitories (-1 2 3 4 5+) comment:________________________

☐ Athletic Center / Gym (-1 2 3 4 5+) comment:________________________

☐ Library (-1 2 3 4 5+) comment:________________________

☐ School Store (-1 2 3 4 5+) comment:________________________

☐ Dining Hall (-1 2 3 4 5+) comment:________________________

☐ Other________________ (-1 2 3 4 5+) comment:________________________

☐ Other________________ (-1 2 3 4 5+) comment:________________________

☐ Other________________ (-1 2 3 4 5+) comment:________________________

How was the food?____

What did I think about the campus and the surrounding area:________________________

____

What did I think about the students and the staff I met? Would I fit in well here? ________________

____

What did I think about the courses of study offered here? Do these meet my goals?________________

____

What did I think about the extracurricular activities offered here? ________________________

OVERALL ASSESSMENT and FOLLOW UP ACTIONS (Page 5 of 6)

Name of College:______________________________

What I like best about this college is:______________________________

What I like least about this college is:______________________________

Follow up actions / next steps I need to do are:______________________________

My overall assessment: (-1 2 3 4 5+) comment:______________________________

My Parents' overall assessment: (-1 2 3 4 5+) comment:______________________________

Additional Notes:

Name of College:____

Page 6 of 6 - STAPLE / ATTACH ANY HANDOUTS, MAPS, ETC HERE:

— —

BEFORE YOU GO (Page 1 of 6)

Name of College:____

Location (Street Address):____

Website URL:_______________________ Phone #:______________________

Type of Visit: ☐ Online (Virtual) / ☐ On Site (Tour) Date of Planned On Site Visit:__________

Size of College: ☐ Small (less than 5,000 students) / ☐ Medium (5,000 to 15,000 students) /
☐ Large (more than 15,000 students)

Type of College: ☐ Liberal Arts / ☐ Science & Engineering / ☐ General Studies
☐ College (Undergraduate only) / ☐ University (Undergraduate & Graduate)
☐ State/Community College / ☐ Private College
☐ 2 Year Undergraduate / ☐ 4 Year Undergraduate

Dates / Times of Tours and Information Sessions:______________________________________

Do I know people who are / will be attending this college? ☐ No / ☐ Yes – Name(s):__________

____

Do I know people who have graduated from this college? ☐ No / ☐ Yes – Name(s):__________

____

I am interested in this college because:________________________________

____

Things I have heard about this college are:______________________________

____

WHEN YOU GET THERE (Page 2 of 6)

Name of College:____

Date of Visit:____________________________ Time of Visit:____________________________

Was school in session when I visited: ☐ Yes / ☐ No

Activities during On Site Visit (check all that apply):

☐ Campus Tour / ☐ Information Session / ☐ Interview / ☐ Tour of Surrounding Area

Surrounding Area: ☐ Rural (Country) / ☐ Suburban (Near residential area) / ☐ Urban (City)

Names of people who presented / people I met with and contact information (phone, email).

____

____

____

Topics discussed at Information Session / notes (see next page for list of possible questions to ask):

____

____

____

____

____

____

____

____

____

____

____

____

WHILE YOU ARE THERE (Page 3 of 6)

Name of College: ______________________________

Questions you can ask (some ideas – feel free to modify these or add more):

- What are entrance requirements (GPA, SAT, SAT2, ACT, AP courses, Honors Courses)? ______________________________
- What is the graduation rate (% of incoming freshmen who will graduate)? ______________
- What percent of classes are taught by professors vs. teaching assistants? ______________
- What is the average class size (Student : Teacher ratio)? ______________
- What is the expected size of the freshman class? ______________
- When is the application deadline (regular and early decision)? ______________________________
- When do I need to declare my major and how easy is it to change? ______________
- Do I need to write a thesis to graduate? ______________
- Do you take transfer credits? ______________
- What learning opportunities are there outside of the classroom (i.e. internships, coop, research programs)? ______________
- How many students typically study abroad? ______________
- Are there fraternities and sororities, and what percent of the students belong to one? ______________
- What are the popular extracurricular activities? ______________
- Is there employment placement assistance for graduating seniors? ______________
- What is the cost for tuition? Room and Board? Books and supplies? ______________
- Is there Financial Aid and/or Scholarships available? How do I apply? ______________
- Can freshman live off campus? Can they have a car on campus? ______________
- Do most students stay on campus over weekends or leave? ______________
- Other questions I have: ______________
- NOTES:

____

____

____

____

____

____

WHAT I LEARNED ABOUT THIS COLLEGE (Page 4 of 6)

Name of College:____

Majors Offered:____

Places I visited during my tour and what I thought of them
Check all that apply and rank from 1 [bad] to 5 [excellent]:

☐ Student Center (-1 2 3 4 5+) comment:____________________

☐ Computer Center (-1 2 3 4 5+) comment:____________________

☐ Labs (-1 2 3 4 5+) comment:____________________

☐ Lecture Halls (-1 2 3 4 5+) comment:____________________

☐ Classrooms (-1 2 3 4 5+) comment:____________________

☐ Department Bldg for my major (-1 2 3 4 5+) comment:____________________

☐ Dormitories (-1 2 3 4 5+) comment:____________________

☐ Athletic Center / Gym (-1 2 3 4 5+) comment:____________________

☐ Library (-1 2 3 4 5+) comment:____________________

☐ School Store (-1 2 3 4 5+) comment:____________________

☐ Dining Hall (-1 2 3 4 5+) comment:____________________

☐ Other________________ (-1 2 3 4 5+) comment:____________________

☐ Other________________ (-1 2 3 4 5+) comment:____________________

☐ Other________________ (-1 2 3 4 5+) comment:____________________

How was the food?____

What did I think about the campus and the surrounding area:____________________

____

What did I think about the students and the staff I met? Would I fit in well here? ________________

____

What did I think about the courses of study offered here? Do these meet my goals?________________

____

What did I think about the extracurricular activities offered here? ____________________

OVERALL ASSESSMENT and FOLLOW UP ACTIONS (Page 5 of 6)

Name of College:____

What I like best about this college is:______________________________

What I like least about this college is:______________________________

Follow up actions / next steps I need to do are:__________________________

My overall assessment: (-1 2 3 4 5+) comment:______________________

My Parents' overall assessment: (-1 2 3 4 5+) comment:_________________

Additional Notes:

Name of College:____

Page 6 of 6 - STAPLE / ATTACH ANY HANDOUTS, MAPS, ETC HERE:

— —

BEFORE YOU GO (Page 1 of 6)

Name of College:____

Location (Street Address):__________________________________

Website URL:________________________ Phone #:________________________

Type of Visit: ☐ Online (Virtual) / ☐ On Site (Tour) Date of Planned On Site Visit:____________

Size of College: ☐ Small (less than 5,000 students) / ☐ Medium (5,000 to 15,000 students) /

☐ Large (more than 15,000 students)

Type of College: ☐ Liberal Arts / ☐ Science & Engineering / ☐ General Studies

☐ College (Undergraduate only) / ☐ University (Undergraduate & Graduate)

☐ State/Community College / ☐ Private College

☐ 2 Year Undergraduate / ☐ 4 Year Undergraduate

Dates / Times of Tours and Information Sessions:____

Do I know people who are / will be attending this college? ☐ No / ☐ Yes – Name(s):______________

____

Do I know people who have graduated from this college? ☐ No / ☐ Yes – Name(s): ____________

____

I am interested in this college because:__________________________________

____

Things I have heard about this college are:________________________________

____

WHEN YOU GET THERE (Page 2 of 6)

Name of College:____

Date of Visit:____________________________ Time of Visit:____________________________

Was school in session when I visited: ☐ Yes / ☐ No

Activities during On Site Visit (check all that apply):

☐ Campus Tour / ☐ Information Session / ☐ Interview / ☐ Tour of Surrounding Area

Surrounding Area: ☐ Rural (Country) / ☐ Suburban (Near residential area) / ☐ Urban (City)

Names of people who presented / people I met with and contact information (phone, email).

____

____

____

Topics discussed at Information Session / notes (see next page for list of possible questions to ask):

____

____

____

____

____

____

____

____

____

____

____

____

WHILE YOU ARE THERE (Page 3 of 6)

Name of College: ______________________________

Questions you can ask (some ideas – feel free to modify these or add more):

- What are entrance requirements (GPA, SAT, SAT2, ACT, AP courses, Honors Courses)? ______________________________
- What is the graduation rate (% of incoming freshmen who will graduate)? ______________
- What percent of classes are taught by professors vs. teaching assistants? ______________
- What is the average class size (Student : Teacher ratio)? ______________
- What is the expected size of the freshman class? ______________
- When is the application deadline (regular and early decision)? ______________________________
- When do I need to declare my major and how easy is it to change? ______________
- Do I need to write a thesis to graduate? ______________
- Do you take transfer credits? ______________
- What learning opportunities are there outside of the classroom (i.e. internships, coop, research programs)? ______________
- How many students typically study abroad? ______________
- Are there fraternities and sororities, and what percent of the students belong to one? ________
- What are the popular extracurricular activities? ______________
- Is there employment placement assistance for graduating seniors? ______________
- What is the cost for tuition? Room and Board? Books and supplies? ______________
- Is there Financial Aid and/or Scholarships available? How do I apply? ______________
- Can freshman live off campus? Can they have a car on campus? ______________
- Do most students stay on campus over weekends or leave? ______________
- Other questions I have: ______________
- NOTES:

____

____

____

____

____

____

WHAT I LEARNED ABOUT THIS COLLEGE (Page 4 of 6)

Name of College:____

Majors Offered:____

Places I visited during my tour and what I thought of them
Check all that apply and rank from 1 [bad] to 5 [excellent]:

☐ Student Center (-1 2 3 4 5+) comment:__________________________

☐ Computer Center (-1 2 3 4 5+) comment:__________________________

☐ Labs (-1 2 3 4 5+) comment:__________________________

☐ Lecture Halls (-1 2 3 4 5+) comment:__________________________

☐ Classrooms (-1 2 3 4 5+) comment:__________________________

☐ Department Bldg for my major (-1 2 3 4 5+) comment:____________________

☐ Dormitories (-1 2 3 4 5+) comment:__________________________

☐ Athletic Center / Gym (-1 2 3 4 5+) comment:________________________

☐ Library (-1 2 3 4 5+) comment:__________________________

☐ School Store (-1 2 3 4 5+) comment:__________________________

☐ Dining Hall (-1 2 3 4 5+) comment:__________________________

☐ Other__________________ (-1 2 3 4 5+) comment:____________________

☐ Other__________________ (-1 2 3 4 5+) comment:____________________

☐ Other__________________ (-1 2 3 4 5+) comment:____________________

How was the food?____

What did I think about the campus and the surrounding area:____________________

____

What did I think about the students and the staff I met? Would I fit in well here? ______________

____

What did I think about the courses of study offered here? Do these meet my goals?______________

____

What did I think about the extracurricular activities offered here? ____________________

OVERALL ASSESSMENT and FOLLOW UP ACTIONS (Page 5 of 6)

Name of College:____

What I like best about this college is:______________________________

What I like least about this college is:______________________________

Follow up actions / next steps I need to do are:__________________________

My overall assessment: (-1 2 3 4 5+) comment:____________________

My Parents' overall assessment: (-1 2 3 4 5+) comment:_________________

Additional Notes:

Name of College:____

Page 6 of 6 - STAPLE / ATTACH ANY HANDOUTS, MAPS, ETC HERE:

— —

BEFORE YOU GO (Page 1 of 6)

Name of College:____

Location (Street Address):____

Website URL:________________________ Phone #:________________________

Type of Visit: ☐ Online (Virtual) / ☐ On Site (Tour) Date of Planned On Site Visit:____________

Size of College: ☐ Small (less than 5,000 students) / ☐ Medium (5,000 to 15,000 students) /

☐ Large (more than 15,000 students)

Type of College: ☐ Liberal Arts / ☐ Science & Engineering / ☐ General Studies

☐ College (Undergraduate only) / ☐ University (Undergraduate & Graduate)

☐ State/Community College / ☐ Private College

☐ 2 Year Undergraduate / ☐ 4 Year Undergraduate

Dates / Times of Tours and Information
Sessions:____

Do I know people who are / will be attending this college? ☐ No / ☐ Yes – Name(s):____________

____

Do I know people who have graduated from this college? ☐ No / ☐ Yes – Name(s):____________

____

I am interested in this college because:____________________________________

____

Things I have heard about this college are:__________________________________

____

WHEN YOU GET THERE (Page 2 of 6)

Name of College:____

Date of Visit:____________________ Time of Visit:____________________

Was school in session when I visited: ☐ Yes / ☐ No

Activities during On Site Visit (check all that apply):

☐ Campus Tour / ☐ Information Session / ☐ Interview / ☐ Tour of Surrounding Area

Surrounding Area: ☐ Rural (Country) / ☐ Suburban (Near residential area) / ☐ Urban (City)

Names of people who presented / people I met with and contact information (phone, email).

Topics discussed at Information Session / notes (see next page for list of possible questions to ask):

WHILE YOU ARE THERE (Page 3 of 6)

Name of College: ____________________

Questions you can ask (some ideas – feel free to modify these or add more):

- What are entrance requirements (GPA, SAT, SAT2, ACT, AP courses, Honors Courses)? ____________________
- What is the graduation rate (% of incoming freshmen who will graduate)? ____________________
- What percent of classes are taught by professors vs. teaching assistants? ____________________
- What is the average class size (Student : Teacher ratio)? ____________________
- What is the expected size of the freshman class? ____________________
- When is the application deadline (regular and early decision)? ____________________
- When do I need to declare my major and how easy is it to change? ____________________
- Do I need to write a thesis to graduate? ____________________
- Do you take transfer credits? ____________________
- What learning opportunities are there outside of the classroom (i.e. internships, coop, research programs)? ____________________
- How many students typically study abroad? ____________________
- Are there fraternities and sororities, and what percent of the students belong to one? ____________________
- What are the popular extracurricular activities? ____________________
- Is there employment placement assistance for graduating seniors? ____________________
- What is the cost for tuition? Room and Board? Books and supplies? ____________________
- Is there Financial Aid and/or Scholarships available? How do I apply? ____________________
- Can freshman live off campus? Can they have a car on campus? ____________________
- Do most students stay on campus over weekends or leave? ____________________
- Other questions I have: ____________________
- NOTES:

____

____

____

____

____

____

WHAT I LEARNED ABOUT THIS COLLEGE (Page 4 of 6)

Name of College:____

Majors Offered:____

Places I visited during my tour and what I thought of them
Check all that apply and rank from 1 [bad] to 5 [excellent]:

☐ Student Center (-1 2 3 4 5+) comment:____________________________

☐ Computer Center (-1 2 3 4 5+) comment:___________________________

☐ Labs (-1 2 3 4 5+) comment:___________________________________

☐ Lecture Halls (-1 2 3 4 5+) comment:_____________________________

☐ Classrooms (-1 2 3 4 5+) comment:_______________________________

☐ Department Bldg for my major (-1 2 3 4 5+) comment:____________________

☐ Dormitories (-1 2 3 4 5+) comment:_______________________________

☐ Athletic Center / Gym (-1 2 3 4 5+) comment:_________________________

☐ Library (-1 2 3 4 5+) comment:__________________________________

☐ School Store (-1 2 3 4 5+) comment:______________________________

☐ Dining Hall (-1 2 3 4 5+) comment:_______________________________

☐ Other________________ (-1 2 3 4 5+) comment:____________________

☐ Other________________ (-1 2 3 4 5+) comment:____________________

☐ Other________________ (-1 2 3 4 5+) comment:____________________

How was the food?____

What did I think about the campus and the surrounding area:____________________________

____

What did I think about the students and the staff I met? Would I fit in well here? ________________

____

What did I think about the courses of study offered here? Do these meet my goals?_______________

____

What did I think about the extracurricular activities offered here? ___________________________

OVERALL ASSESSMENT and FOLLOW UP ACTIONS (Page 5 of 6)

Name of College:____

What I like best about this college is:______________________________

What I like least about this college is:______________________________

Follow up actions / next steps I need to do are:__________________________

My overall assessment: (-1 2 3 4 5+) comment:______________________

My Parents' overall assessment: (-1 2 3 4 5+) comment:__________________

Additional Notes:

Name of College:____

Page 6 of 6 - STAPLE / ATTACH ANY HANDOUTS, MAPS, ETC HERE:

— —

BEFORE YOU GO (Page 1 of 6)

Name of College:____

Location (Street Address):____

Website URL:________________________ Phone #:________________________

Type of Visit: ☐ Online (Virtual) / ☐ On Site (Tour) Date of Planned On Site Visit:____________

Size of College: ☐ Small (less than 5,000 students) / ☐ Medium (5,000 to 15,000 students) /

☐ Large (more than 15,000 students)

Type of College: ☐ Liberal Arts / ☐ Science & Engineering / ☐ General Studies

☐ College (Undergraduate only) / ☐ University (Undergraduate & Graduate)

☐ State/Community College / ☐ Private College

☐ 2 Year Undergraduate / ☐ 4 Year Undergraduate

Dates / Times of Tours and Information Sessions:____

Do I know people who are / will be attending this college? ☐ No / ☐ Yes – Name(s):____________

____

Do I know people who have graduated from this college? ☐ No / ☐ Yes – Name(s):____________

____

I am interested in this college because:____________________________________

____

Things I have heard about this college are:__________________________________

____

WHEN YOU GET THERE (Page 2 of 6)

Name of College:____

Date of Visit:___________________________ Time of Visit:___________________________

Was school in session when I visited: ☐ Yes / ☐ No

Activities during On Site Visit (check all that apply):

☐ Campus Tour / ☐ Information Session / ☐ Interview / ☐ Tour of Surrounding Area

Surrounding Area: ☐ Rural (Country) / ☐ Suburban (Near residential area) / ☐ Urban (City)

Names of people who presented / people I met with and contact information (phone, email).

____

____

____

Topics discussed at Information Session / notes (see next page for list of possible questions to ask):

____

____

____

____

____

____

____

____

____

____

____

____

WHILE YOU ARE THERE (Page 3 of 6)

Name of College: ____________________

Questions you can ask (some ideas – feel free to modify these or add more):

- What are entrance requirements (GPA, SAT, SAT2, ACT, AP courses, Honors Courses)?
  ____
- What is the graduation rate (% of incoming freshmen who will graduate)? ____________________
- What percent of classes are taught by professors vs. teaching assistants? ____________________
- What is the average class size (Student : Teacher ratio)? ____________________
- What is the expected size of the freshman class? ____________________
- When is the application deadline (regular and early decision)?
  ____
- When do I need to declare my major and how easy is it to change? ____________________
- Do I need to write a thesis to graduate? ____________________
- Do you take transfer credits? ____________________
- What learning opportunities are there outside of the classroom (i.e. internships, coop, research programs)? ____________________
- How many students typically study abroad? ____________________
- Are there fraternities and sororities, and what percent of the students belong to one? ____________________
- What are the popular extracurricular activities? ____________________
- Is there employment placement assistance for graduating seniors? ____________________
- What is the cost for tuition? Room and Board? Books and supplies? ____________________
- Is there Financial Aid and/or Scholarships available? How do I apply? ____________________
- Can freshman live off campus? Can they have a car on campus? ____________________
- Do most students stay on campus over weekends or leave? ____________________
- Other questions I have: ____________________
- NOTES:

____

____

____

____

____

____

WHAT I LEARNED ABOUT THIS COLLEGE (Page 4 of 6)

Name of College:____

Majors Offered:____

Places I visited during my tour and what I thought of them
Check all that apply and rank from 1 [bad] to 5 [excellent]:

☐ Student Center (-1 2 3 4 5+) comment:____________________________

☐ Computer Center (-1 2 3 4 5+) comment:____________________________

☐ Labs (-1 2 3 4 5+) comment:____________________________

☐ Lecture Halls (-1 2 3 4 5+) comment:____________________________

☐ Classrooms (-1 2 3 4 5+) comment:____________________________

☐ Department Bldg for my major (-1 2 3 4 5+) comment:____________________

☐ Dormitories (-1 2 3 4 5+) comment:____________________________

☐ Athletic Center / Gym (-1 2 3 4 5+) comment:________________________

☐ Library (-1 2 3 4 5+) comment:____________________________

☐ School Store (-1 2 3 4 5+) comment:____________________________

☐ Dining Hall (-1 2 3 4 5+) comment:____________________________

☐ Other________________ (-1 2 3 4 5+) comment:____________________

☐ Other________________ (-1 2 3 4 5+) comment:____________________

☐ Other________________ (-1 2 3 4 5+) comment:____________________

How was the food?____

What did I think about the campus and the surrounding area:____________________

____

What did I think about the students and the staff I met? Would I fit in well here? ________________

____

What did I think about the courses of study offered here? Do these meet my goals?________________

____

What did I think about the extracurricular activities offered here? ____________________

OVERALL ASSESSMENT and FOLLOW UP ACTIONS (Page 5 of 6)

Name of College:____

What I like best about this college is:________________________________

What I like least about this college is:________________________________

Follow up actions / next steps I need to do are:__________________________

My overall assessment: (-1 2 3 4 5+) comment:______________________

My Parents' overall assessment: (-1 2 3 4 5+) comment:__________________

Additional Notes:

Name of College:____

Page 6 of 6 - STAPLE / ATTACH ANY HANDOUTS, MAPS, ETC HERE:

— —

BEFORE YOU GO (Page 1 of 6)

Name of College:____

Location (Street Address):____

Website URL:________________________ Phone #:________________________

Type of Visit: ☐ Online (Virtual) / ☐ On Site (Tour) Date of Planned On Site Visit:__________

Size of College: ☐ Small (less than 5,000 students) / ☐ Medium (5,000 to 15,000 students) /
☐ Large (more than 15,000 students)

Type of College: ☐ Liberal Arts / ☐ Science & Engineering / ☐ General Studies
☐ College (Undergraduate only) / ☐ University (Undergraduate & Graduate)
☐ State/Community College / ☐ Private College
☐ 2 Year Undergraduate / ☐ 4 Year Undergraduate

Dates / Times of Tours and Information
Sessions:____

Do I know people who are / will be attending this college? ☐ No / ☐ Yes – Name(s):__________

____

Do I know people who have graduated from this college? ☐ No / ☐ Yes – Name(s):__________

____

I am interested in this college because:________________________________

____

Things I have heard about this college are:______________________________

____

WHEN YOU GET THERE (Page 2 of 6)

Name of College:____

Date of Visit:____________________ Time of Visit:____________________

Was school in session when I visited: ☐ Yes / ☐ No

Activities during On Site Visit (check all that apply):

☐ Campus Tour / ☐ Information Session / ☐ Interview / ☐ Tour of Surrounding Area

Surrounding Area: ☐ Rural (Country) / ☐ Suburban (Near residential area) / ☐ Urban (City)

Names of people who presented / people I met with and contact information (phone, email).

Topics discussed at Information Session / notes (see next page for list of possible questions to ask):

WHILE YOU ARE THERE (Page 3 of 6)

Name of College: ____

Questions you can ask (some ideas – feel free to modify these or add more):

- What are entrance requirements (GPA, SAT, SAT2, ACT, AP courses, Honors Courses)? ____
- What is the graduation rate (% of incoming freshmen who will graduate)? ____________
- What percent of classes are taught by professors vs. teaching assistants? ____________
- What is the average class size (Student : Teacher ratio)? ____________________
- What is the expected size of the freshman class? ________________________
- When is the application deadline (regular and early decision)? ____
- When do I need to declare my major and how easy is it to change? ______________
- Do I need to write a thesis to graduate? ____________________________
- Do you take transfer credits? ________________________________
- What learning opportunities are there outside of the classroom (i.e. internships, coop, research programs)? ____________________________________
- How many students typically study abroad? __________________________
- Are there fraternities and sororities, and what percent of the students belong to one? _______
- What are the popular extracurricular activities? ________________________
- Is there employment placement assistance for graduating seniors? ______________
- What is the cost for tuition? Room and Board? Books and supplies? ______________
- Is there Financial Aid and/or Scholarships available? How do I apply? ______________
- Can freshman live off campus? Can they have a car on campus? ________________
- Do most students stay on campus over weekends or leave? ____________________
- Other questions I have: ____________________________________
- NOTES:

WHAT I LEARNED ABOUT THIS COLLEGE (Page 4 of 6)

Name of College:____

Majors Offered:____

Places I visited during my tour and what I thought of them
Check all that apply and rank from 1 [bad] to 5 [excellent]:

☐ Student Center (-1 2 3 4 5+) comment:__________________________

☐ Computer Center (-1 2 3 4 5+) comment:__________________________

☐ Labs (-1 2 3 4 5+) comment:__________________________________

☐ Lecture Halls (-1 2 3 4 5+) comment:____________________________

☐ Classrooms (-1 2 3 4 5+) comment:______________________________

☐ Department Bldg for my major (-1 2 3 4 5+) comment:__________________

☐ Dormitories (-1 2 3 4 5+) comment:______________________________

☐ Athletic Center / Gym (-1 2 3 4 5+) comment:________________________

☐ Library (-1 2 3 4 5+) comment:________________________________

☐ School Store (-1 2 3 4 5+) comment:_____________________________

☐ Dining Hall (-1 2 3 4 5+) comment:______________________________

☐ Other__________________ (-1 2 3 4 5+) comment:__________________

☐ Other__________________ (-1 2 3 4 5+) comment:__________________

☐ Other__________________ (-1 2 3 4 5+) comment:__________________

How was the food?____

What did I think about the campus and the surrounding area:_____________________

____

What did I think about the students and the staff I met? Would I fit in well here? ______________

____

What did I think about the courses of study offered here? Do these meet my goals?______________

____

What did I think about the extracurricular activities offered here? ______________________

OVERALL ASSESSMENT and FOLLOW UP ACTIONS (Page 5 of 6)

Name of College:____

What I like best about this college is:______________________________

What I like least about this college is:______________________________

Follow up actions / next steps I need to do are:__________________________

My overall assessment: (-1 2 3 4 5+) comment:____________________

My Parents' overall assessment: (-1 2 3 4 5+) comment:________________

Additional Notes:

Name of College:____

Page 6 of 6 - STAPLE / ATTACH ANY HANDOUTS, MAPS, ETC HERE:

— —

BEFORE YOU GO (Page 1 of 6)

Name of College:____

Location (Street Address):_______________________________________

Website URL:_______________________ Phone #:______________________

Type of Visit: ☐ Online (Virtual) / ☐ On Site (Tour) Date of Planned On Site Visit:__________

Size of College: ☐ Small (less than 5,000 students) / ☐ Medium (5,000 to 15,000 students) /

☐ Large (more than 15,000 students)

Type of College: ☐ Liberal Arts / ☐ Science & Engineering / ☐ General Studies

☐ College (Undergraduate only) / ☐ University (Undergraduate & Graduate)

☐ State/Community College / ☐ Private College

☐ 2 Year Undergraduate / ☐ 4 Year Undergraduate

Dates / Times of Tours and Information Sessions:____

Do I know people who are / will be attending this college? ☐ No / ☐ Yes – Name(s):__________

____

Do I know people who have graduated from this college? ☐ No / ☐ Yes – Name(s):__________

____

I am interested in this college because:____________________________________

____

Things I have heard about this college are:_________________________________

____

WHEN YOU GET THERE (Page 2 of 6)

Name of College:____

Date of Visit:____________________ Time of Visit:____________________

Was school in session when I visited: ☐ Yes / ☐ No

Activities during On Site Visit (check all that apply):

☐ Campus Tour / ☐ Information Session / ☐ Interview / ☐ Tour of Surrounding Area

Surrounding Area: ☐ Rural (Country) / ☐ Suburban (Near residential area) / ☐ Urban (City)

Names of people who presented / people I met with and contact information (phone, email).

____

____

____

Topics discussed at Information Session / notes (see next page for list of possible questions to ask):

____

____

____

____

____

____

____

____

____

____

____

____

WHILE YOU ARE THERE (Page 3 of 6)

Name of College: ______________________________

Questions you can ask (some ideas – feel free to modify these or add more):

- What are entrance requirements (GPA, SAT, SAT2, ACT, AP courses, Honors Courses)? ______________________________
- What is the graduation rate (% of incoming freshmen who will graduate)? ______________
- What percent of classes are taught by professors vs. teaching assistants? ______________
- What is the average class size (Student : Teacher ratio)? ______________
- What is the expected size of the freshman class? ______________
- When is the application deadline (regular and early decision)? ______________________________
- When do I need to declare my major and how easy is it to change? ______________
- Do I need to write a thesis to graduate? ______________
- Do you take transfer credits? ______________
- What learning opportunities are there outside of the classroom (i.e. internships, coop, research programs)? ______________
- How many students typically study abroad? ______________
- Are there fraternities and sororities, and what percent of the students belong to one? ________
- What are the popular extracurricular activities? ______________
- Is there employment placement assistance for graduating seniors? ______________
- What is the cost for tuition? Room and Board? Books and supplies? ______________
- Is there Financial Aid and/or Scholarships available? How do I apply? ______________
- Can freshman live off campus? Can they have a car on campus? ______________
- Do most students stay on campus over weekends or leave? ______________
- Other questions I have: ______________
- NOTES:

____

____

____

____

____

____

WHAT I LEARNED ABOUT THIS COLLEGE (Page 4 of 6)

Name of College:____

Majors Offered:____

Places I visited during my tour and what I thought of them
Check all that apply and rank from 1 [bad] to 5 [excellent]:

☐ Student Center (-1 2 3 4 5+) comment:__________________________

☐ Computer Center (-1 2 3 4 5+) comment:__________________________

☐ Labs (-1 2 3 4 5+) comment:__________________________

☐ Lecture Halls (-1 2 3 4 5+) comment:__________________________

☐ Classrooms (-1 2 3 4 5+) comment:__________________________

☐ Department Bldg for my major (-1 2 3 4 5+) comment:__________________________

☐ Dormitories (-1 2 3 4 5+) comment:__________________________

☐ Athletic Center / Gym (-1 2 3 4 5+) comment:__________________________

☐ Library (-1 2 3 4 5+) comment:__________________________

☐ School Store (-1 2 3 4 5+) comment:__________________________

☐ Dining Hall (-1 2 3 4 5+) comment:__________________________

☐ Other________________ (-1 2 3 4 5+) comment:__________________________

☐ Other________________ (-1 2 3 4 5+) comment:__________________________

☐ Other________________ (-1 2 3 4 5+) comment:__________________________

How was the food?____

What did I think about the campus and the surrounding area:__________________________

____

What did I think about the students and the staff I met? Would I fit in well here? ________________

____

What did I think about the courses of study offered here? Do these meet my goals?________________

____

What did I think about the extracurricular activities offered here? __________________________

OVERALL ASSESSMENT and FOLLOW UP ACTIONS (Page 5 of 6)

Name of College:____

What I like best about this college is:______________________________

What I like least about this college is:______________________________

Follow up actions / next steps I need to do are:__________________________

My overall assessment: (-1 2 3 4 5+) comment:______________________

My Parents' overall assessment: (-1 2 3 4 5+) comment:_________________

Additional Notes:

Name of College:____

Page 6 of 6 - STAPLE / ATTACH ANY HANDOUTS, MAPS, ETC HERE:

— —

BEFORE YOU GO (Page 1 of 6)

Name of College:____

Location (Street Address):____

Website URL:________________________ Phone #:________________________

Type of Visit: ☐ Online (Virtual) / ☐ On Site (Tour) Date of Planned On Site Visit:____________

Size of College: ☐ Small (less than 5,000 students) / ☐ Medium (5,000 to 15,000 students) /

☐ Large (more than 15,000 students)

Type of College: ☐ Liberal Arts / ☐ Science & Engineering / ☐ General Studies

☐ College (Undergraduate only) / ☐ University (Undergraduate & Graduate)

☐ State/Community College / ☐ Private College

☐ 2 Year Undergraduate / ☐ 4 Year Undergraduate

Dates / Times of Tours and Information
Sessions:____

Do I know people who are / will be attending this college? ☐ No / ☐ Yes – Name(s):____________

____

Do I know people who have graduated from this college? ☐ No / ☐ Yes – Name(s):____________

____

I am interested in this college because:____________________________________

____

Things I have heard about this college are:__________________________________

____

WHEN YOU GET THERE (Page 2 of 6)

Name of College:____

Date of Visit:____________________ Time of Visit:____________________

Was school in session when I visited: ☐ Yes / ☐ No

Activities during On Site Visit (check all that apply):

☐ Campus Tour / ☐ Information Session / ☐ Interview / ☐ Tour of Surrounding Area

Surrounding Area: ☐ Rural (Country) / ☐ Suburban (Near residential area) / ☐ Urban (City)

Names of people who presented / people I met with and contact information (phone, email).

Topics discussed at Information Session / notes (see next page for list of possible questions to ask):

WHILE YOU ARE THERE (Page 3 of 6)

Name of College:____

Questions you can ask (some ideas – feel free to modify these or add more):

- What are entrance requirements (GPA, SAT, SAT2, ACT, AP courses, Honors Courses)? ____
- What is the graduation rate (% of incoming freshmen who will graduate)? ______________
- What percent of classes are taught by professors vs. teaching assistants? ______________
- What is the average class size (Student : Teacher ratio)? ____________________
- What is the expected size of the freshman class? ________________________
- When is the application deadline (regular and early decision)? ____
- When do I need to declare my major and how easy is it to change? _______________
- Do I need to write a thesis to graduate? ____________________________
- Do you take transfer credits? _________________________________
- What learning opportunities are there outside of the classroom (i.e. internships, coop, research programs)? ____
- How many students typically study abroad? __________________________
- Are there fraternities and sororities, and what percent of the students belong to one? ________
- What are the popular extracurricular activities? ________________________
- Is there employment placement assistance for graduating seniors? ________________
- What is the cost for tuition? Room and Board? Books and supplies? _______________
- Is there Financial Aid and/or Scholarships available? How do I apply? _______________
- Can freshman live off campus? Can they have a car on campus? _________________
- Do most students stay on campus over weekends or leave? ____________________
- Other questions I have: ______________________________________
- NOTES:

____

____

____

____

____

____

WHAT I LEARNED ABOUT THIS COLLEGE (Page 4 of 6)

Name of College:____

Majors Offered:____

Places I visited during my tour and what I thought of them
Check all that apply and rank from 1 [bad] to 5 [excellent]:

☐ Student Center (-1 2 3 4 5+) comment:______________________________

☐ Computer Center (-1 2 3 4 5+) comment:______________________________

☐ Labs (-1 2 3 4 5+) comment:______________________________

☐ Lecture Halls (-1 2 3 4 5+) comment:______________________________

☐ Classrooms (-1 2 3 4 5+) comment:______________________________

☐ Department Bldg for my major (-1 2 3 4 5+) comment:____________________

☐ Dormitories (-1 2 3 4 5+) comment:______________________________

☐ Athletic Center / Gym (-1 2 3 4 5+) comment:______________________________

☐ Library (-1 2 3 4 5+) comment:______________________________

☐ School Store (-1 2 3 4 5+) comment:______________________________

☐ Dining Hall (-1 2 3 4 5+) comment:______________________________

☐ Other____________________ (-1 2 3 4 5+) comment:____________________

☐ Other____________________ (-1 2 3 4 5+) comment:____________________

☐ Other____________________ (-1 2 3 4 5+) comment:____________________

How was the food?____

What did I think about the campus and the surrounding area:______________________________

____

What did I think about the students and the staff I met? Would I fit in well here? ____________________

____

What did I think about the courses of study offered here? Do these meet my goals?____________________

____

What did I think about the extracurricular activities offered here? ______________________________

OVERALL ASSESSMENT and FOLLOW UP ACTIONS (Page 5 of 6)

Name of College:____

What I like best about this college is:______________________________________

____

____

____

What I like least about this college is:______________________________________

____

____

____

Follow up actions / next steps I need to do are:______________________________

____

____

____

My overall assessment: (-1 2 3 4 5+) comment:______________________

My Parents' overall assessment: (-1 2 3 4 5+) comment:__________________

Additional Notes:

____

____

____

____

____

____

____

____

____

____

____

____

Name of College:____

Page 6 of 6 - STAPLE / ATTACH ANY HANDOUTS, MAPS, ETC HERE:

— —

BEFORE YOU GO (Page 1 of 6)

Name of College:____

Location (Street Address):____

Website URL:_____________________________ Phone #:___________________________

Type of Visit: ☐ Online (Virtual) / ☐ On Site (Tour) Date of Planned On Site Visit:____________

Size of College: ☐ Small (less than 5,000 students) / ☐ Medium (5,000 to 15,000 students) /

☐ Large (more than 15,000 students)

Type of College: ☐ Liberal Arts / ☐ Science & Engineering / ☐ General Studies

☐ College (Undergraduate only) / ☐ University (Undergraduate & Graduate)

☐ State/Community College / ☐ Private College

☐ 2 Year Undergraduate / ☐ 4 Year Undergraduate

Dates / Times of Tours and Information Sessions:____

Do I know people who are / will be attending this college? ☐ No / ☐ Yes – Name(s):____________

____

Do I know people who have graduated from this college? ☐ No / ☐ Yes – Name(s):_____________

____

I am interested in this college because:____

____

Things I have heard about this college are:____

____

WHEN YOU GET THERE (Page 2 of 6)

Name of College:____

Date of Visit:____________________ Time of Visit:____________________

Was school in session when I visited: ☐ Yes / ☐ No

Activities during On Site Visit (check all that apply):

☐ Campus Tour / ☐ Information Session / ☐ Interview / ☐ Tour of Surrounding Area

Surrounding Area: ☐ Rural (Country) / ☐ Suburban (Near residential area) / ☐ Urban (City)

Names of people who presented / people I met with and contact information (phone, email).

____

____

____

Topics discussed at Information Session / notes (see next page for list of possible questions to ask):

____

____

____

____

____

____

____

____

____

____

____

____

WHILE YOU ARE THERE (Page 3 of 6)

Name of College: ____________________

Questions you can ask (some ideas – feel free to modify these or add more):

- What are entrance requirements (GPA, SAT, SAT2, ACT, AP courses, Honors Courses)? ____________________
- What is the graduation rate (% of incoming freshmen who will graduate)? ____________________
- What percent of classes are taught by professors vs. teaching assistants? ____________________
- What is the average class size (Student : Teacher ratio)? ____________________
- What is the expected size of the freshman class? ____________________
- When is the application deadline (regular and early decision)? ____________________
- When do I need to declare my major and how easy is it to change? ____________________
- Do I need to write a thesis to graduate? ____________________
- Do you take transfer credits? ____________________
- What learning opportunities are there outside of the classroom (i.e. internships, coop, research programs)? ____________________
- How many students typically study abroad? ____________________
- Are there fraternities and sororities, and what percent of the students belong to one? ____________________
- What are the popular extracurricular activities? ____________________
- Is there employment placement assistance for graduating seniors? ____________________
- What is the cost for tuition? Room and Board? Books and supplies? ____________________
- Is there Financial Aid and/or Scholarships available? How do I apply? ____________________
- Can freshman live off campus? Can they have a car on campus? ____________________
- Do most students stay on campus over weekends or leave? ____________________
- Other questions I have: ____________________
- NOTES:

____

____

____

____

____

____

WHAT I LEARNED ABOUT THIS COLLEGE (Page 4 of 6)

Name of College:____

Majors Offered:____

Places I visited during my tour and what I thought of them
Check all that apply and rank from 1 [bad] to 5 [excellent]:

☐ Student Center (-1 2 3 4 5+) comment:______________________

☐ Computer Center (-1 2 3 4 5+) comment:______________________

☐ Labs (-1 2 3 4 5+) comment:______________________

☐ Lecture Halls (-1 2 3 4 5+) comment:______________________

☐ Classrooms (-1 2 3 4 5+) comment:______________________

☐ Department Bldg for my major (-1 2 3 4 5+) comment:______________________

☐ Dormitories (-1 2 3 4 5+) comment:______________________

☐ Athletic Center / Gym (-1 2 3 4 5+) comment:______________________

☐ Library (-1 2 3 4 5+) comment:______________________

☐ School Store (-1 2 3 4 5+) comment:______________________

☐ Dining Hall (-1 2 3 4 5+) comment:______________________

☐ Other______________ (-1 2 3 4 5+) comment:______________________

☐ Other______________ (-1 2 3 4 5+) comment:______________________

☐ Other______________ (-1 2 3 4 5+) comment:______________________

How was the food?____

What did I think about the campus and the surrounding area:______________________

____

What did I think about the students and the staff I met? Would I fit in well here? ______________

____

What did I think about the courses of study offered here? Do these meet my goals?______________

____

What did I think about the extracurricular activities offered here? ______________________

OVERALL ASSESSMENT and FOLLOW UP ACTIONS (Page 5 of 6)

Name of College:____

What I like best about this college is:______________________________

What I like least about this college is:______________________________

Follow up actions / next steps I need to do are:__________________________

My overall assessment: (-1 2 3 4 5+) comment:____________________

My Parents' overall assessment: (-1 2 3 4 5+) comment:________________

Additional Notes:

Name of College:____

Page 6 of 6 - STAPLE / ATTACH ANY HANDOUTS, MAPS, ETC HERE:

— —

BEFORE YOU GO (Page 1 of 6)

Name of College:____

Location (Street Address):____________________________________

Website URL:____________________ Phone #:____________________

Type of Visit: ☐ Online (Virtual) / ☐ On Site (Tour) Date of Planned On Site Visit:__________

Size of College: ☐ Small (less than 5,000 students) / ☐ Medium (5,000 to 15,000 students) /

☐ Large (more than 15,000 students)

Type of College: ☐ Liberal Arts / ☐ Science & Engineering / ☐ General Studies

☐ College (Undergraduate only) / ☐ University (Undergraduate & Graduate)

☐ State/Community College / ☐ Private College

☐ 2 Year Undergraduate / ☐ 4 Year Undergraduate

Dates / Times of Tours and Information Sessions:____________________________________

Do I know people who are / will be attending this college? ☐ No / ☐ Yes – Name(s):__________

____

Do I know people who have graduated from this college? ☐ No / ☐ Yes – Name(s):__________

____

I am interested in this college because:__________________________________

____

Things I have heard about this college are:_______________________________

____

WHEN YOU GET THERE (Page 2 of 6)

Name of College:____

Date of Visit:____________________ Time of Visit:____________________

Was school in session when I visited: ☐ Yes / ☐ No

Activities during On Site Visit (check all that apply):

☐ Campus Tour / ☐ Information Session / ☐ Interview / ☐ Tour of Surrounding Area

Surrounding Area: ☐ Rural (Country) / ☐ Suburban (Near residential area) / ☐ Urban (City)

Names of people who presented / people I met with and contact information (phone, email).

____

____

____

Topics discussed at Information Session / notes (see next page for list of possible questions to ask):

WHILE YOU ARE THERE (Page 3 of 6)

Name of College:____

Questions you can ask (some ideas – feel free to modify these or add more):

- What are entrance requirements (GPA, SAT, SAT2, ACT, AP courses, Honors Courses)? ____________________
- What is the graduation rate (% of incoming freshmen who will graduate)? __________
- What percent of classes are taught by professors vs. teaching assistants? __________
- What is the average class size (Student : Teacher ratio)? __________
- What is the expected size of the freshman class? __________
- When is the application deadline (regular and early decision)? ____________________
- When do I need to declare my major and how easy is it to change? __________
- Do I need to write a thesis to graduate? __________
- Do you take transfer credits? __________
- What learning opportunities are there outside of the classroom (i.e. internships, coop, research programs)? __________
- How many students typically study abroad? __________
- Are there fraternities and sororities, and what percent of the students belong to one? __________
- What are the popular extracurricular activities? __________
- Is there employment placement assistance for graduating seniors? __________
- What is the cost for tuition? Room and Board? Books and supplies? __________
- Is there Financial Aid and/or Scholarships available? How do I apply? __________
- Can freshman live off campus? Can they have a car on campus? __________
- Do most students stay on campus over weekends or leave? __________
- Other questions I have: __________
- NOTES:

WHAT I LEARNED ABOUT THIS COLLEGE (Page 4 of 6)

Name of College:____

Majors Offered:____

Places I visited during my tour and what I thought of them
Check all that apply and rank from 1 [bad] to 5 [excellent]:

☐ Student Center (-1 2 3 4 5+) comment:____________________

☐ Computer Center (-1 2 3 4 5+) comment:____________________

☐ Labs (-1 2 3 4 5+) comment:____________________

☐ Lecture Halls (-1 2 3 4 5+) comment:____________________

☐ Classrooms (-1 2 3 4 5+) comment:____________________

☐ Department Bldg for my major (-1 2 3 4 5+) comment:____________________

☐ Dormitories (-1 2 3 4 5+) comment:____________________

☐ Athletic Center / Gym (-1 2 3 4 5+) comment:____________________

☐ Library (-1 2 3 4 5+) comment:____________________

☐ School Store (-1 2 3 4 5+) comment:____________________

☐ Dining Hall (-1 2 3 4 5+) comment:____________________

☐ Other________________ (-1 2 3 4 5+) comment:____________________

☐ Other________________ (-1 2 3 4 5+) comment:____________________

☐ Other________________ (-1 2 3 4 5+) comment:____________________

How was the food?____

What did I think about the campus and the surrounding area:____________________

____

What did I think about the students and the staff I met? Would I fit in well here? ________________

____

What did I think about the courses of study offered here? Do these meet my goals?________________

____

What did I think about the extracurricular activities offered here? ____________________

OVERALL ASSESSMENT and FOLLOW UP ACTIONS (Page 5 of 6)

Name of College:____

What I like best about this college is:______________________________

What I like least about this college is:______________________________

Follow up actions / next steps I need to do are:__________________________

My overall assessment: (-1 2 3 4 5+) comment:____________________

My Parents' overall assessment: (-1 2 3 4 5+) comment:________________

Additional Notes:

Name of College:____

Page 6 of 6 - STAPLE / ATTACH ANY HANDOUTS, MAPS, ETC HERE:

— —

BEFORE YOU GO (Page 1 of 6)

Name of College:____

Location (Street Address):____

Website URL:____________________ Phone #:____________________

Type of Visit: ☐ Online (Virtual) / ☐ On Site (Tour) Date of Planned On Site Visit:__________

Size of College: ☐ Small (less than 5,000 students) / ☐ Medium (5,000 to 15,000 students) /
☐ Large (more than 15,000 students)

Type of College: ☐ Liberal Arts / ☐ Science & Engineering / ☐ General Studies
☐ College (Undergraduate only) / ☐ University (Undergraduate & Graduate)
☐ State/Community College / ☐ Private College
☐ 2 Year Undergraduate / ☐ 4 Year Undergraduate

Dates / Times of Tours and Information Sessions:____

Do I know people who are / will be attending this college? ☐ No / ☐ Yes – Name(s):__________

____

Do I know people who have graduated from this college? ☐ No / ☐ Yes – Name(s):__________

____

I am interested in this college because:________________________________

____

Things I have heard about this college are:______________________________

____

WHEN YOU GET THERE (Page 2 of 6)

Name of College:____

Date of Visit:____________________ Time of Visit:____________________

Was school in session when I visited: ☐ Yes / ☐ No

Activities during On Site Visit (check all that apply):

☐ Campus Tour / ☐ Information Session / ☐ Interview / ☐ Tour of Surrounding Area

Surrounding Area: ☐ Rural (Country) / ☐ Suburban (Near residential area) / ☐ Urban (City)

Names of people who presented / people I met with and contact information (phone, email).

____

____

____

Topics discussed at Information Session / notes (see next page for list of possible questions to ask):

____

____

____

____

____

____

____

____

____

____

____

____

WHILE YOU ARE THERE (Page 3 of 6)

Name of College:____

Questions you can ask (some ideas – feel free to modify these or add more):

- What are entrance requirements (GPA, SAT, SAT2, ACT, AP courses, Honors Courses)? ____
- What is the graduation rate (% of incoming freshmen who will graduate)? __________
- What percent of classes are taught by professors vs. teaching assistants? __________
- What is the average class size (Student : Teacher ratio)? ________________
- What is the expected size of the freshman class? ____________________
- When is the application deadline (regular and early decision)? ____
- When do I need to declare my major and how easy is it to change? ____________
- Do I need to write a thesis to graduate? __________________________
- Do you take transfer credits? ______________________________
- What learning opportunities are there outside of the classroom (i.e. internships, coop, research programs)? ____________________________________
- How many students typically study abroad? ______________________
- Are there fraternities and sororities, and what percent of the students belong to one? ______
- What are the popular extracurricular activities? ____________________
- Is there employment placement assistance for graduating seniors? ____________
- What is the cost for tuition? Room and Board? Books and supplies? ____________
- Is there Financial Aid and/or Scholarships available? How do I apply? ____________
- Can freshman live off campus? Can they have a car on campus? ______________
- Do most students stay on campus over weekends or leave? _______________
- Other questions I have: _________________________________
- NOTES:

WHAT I LEARNED ABOUT THIS COLLEGE (Page 4 of 6)

Name of College:____

Majors Offered:____

Places I visited during my tour and what I thought of them
Check all that apply and rank from 1 [bad] to 5 [excellent]:

☐ Student Center (-1 2 3 4 5+) comment:________________________

☐ Computer Center (-1 2 3 4 5+) comment:________________________

☐ Labs (-1 2 3 4 5+) comment:________________________

☐ Lecture Halls (-1 2 3 4 5+) comment:________________________

☐ Classrooms (-1 2 3 4 5+) comment:________________________

☐ Department Bldg for my major (-1 2 3 4 5+) comment:________________

☐ Dormitories (-1 2 3 4 5+) comment:________________________

☐ Athletic Center / Gym (-1 2 3 4 5+) comment:____________________

☐ Library (-1 2 3 4 5+) comment:________________________

☐ School Store (-1 2 3 4 5+) comment:________________________

☐ Dining Hall (-1 2 3 4 5+) comment:________________________

☐ Other________________ (-1 2 3 4 5+) comment:________________

☐ Other________________ (-1 2 3 4 5+) comment:________________

☐ Other________________ (-1 2 3 4 5+) comment:________________

How was the food?____

What did I think about the campus and the surrounding area:________________

____

What did I think about the students and the staff I met? Would I fit in well here? ____________

____

What did I think about the courses of study offered here? Do these meet my goals?____________

____

What did I think about the extracurricular activities offered here? ________________

OVERALL ASSESSMENT and FOLLOW UP ACTIONS (Page 5 of 6)

Name of College:____________________________________

What I like best about this college is:____________________________

What I like least about this college is:____________________________

Follow up actions / next steps I need to do are:________________________

My overall assessment: (-1 2 3 4 5+) comment:____________________

My Parents' overall assessment: (-1 2 3 4 5+) comment:________________

Additional Notes:

Name of College:____

Page 6 of 6 - STAPLE / ATTACH ANY HANDOUTS, MAPS, ETC HERE:

— —

BEFORE YOU GO (Page 1 of 6)

Name of College:____

Location (Street Address):________________________________

Website URL:____________________ Phone #:____________________

Type of Visit: ☐ Online (Virtual) / ☐ On Site (Tour) Date of Planned On Site Visit:________

Size of College: ☐ Small (less than 5,000 students) / ☐ Medium (5,000 to 15,000 students) /
☐ Large (more than 15,000 students)

Type of College: ☐ Liberal Arts / ☐ Science & Engineering / ☐ General Studies
☐ College (Undergraduate only) / ☐ University (Undergraduate & Graduate)
☐ State/Community College / ☐ Private College
☐ 2 Year Undergraduate / ☐ 4 Year Undergraduate

Dates / Times of Tours and Information Sessions:____

Do I know people who are / will be attending this college? ☐ No / ☐ Yes – Name(s):__________

____

Do I know people who have graduated from this college? ☐ No / ☐ Yes – Name(s):__________

____

I am interested in this college because:________________________________

____

Things I have heard about this college are:______________________________

____

WHEN YOU GET THERE (Page 2 of 6)

Name of College:____

Date of Visit:________________________ Time of Visit:________________________

Was school in session when I visited: ☐ Yes / ☐ No

Activities during On Site Visit (check all that apply):

☐ Campus Tour / ☐ Information Session / ☐ Interview / ☐ Tour of Surrounding Area

Surrounding Area: ☐ Rural (Country) / ☐ Suburban (Near residential area) / ☐ Urban (City)

Names of people who presented / people I met with and contact information (phone, email).

____

____

____

Topics discussed at Information Session / notes (see next page for list of possible questions to ask):

____

____

____

____

____

____

____

____

____

____

____

____

WHILE YOU ARE THERE (Page 3 of 6)

Name of College:____

Questions you can ask (some ideas – feel free to modify these or add more):

- What are entrance requirements (GPA, SAT, SAT2, ACT, AP courses, Honors Courses)? ____
- What is the graduation rate (% of incoming freshmen who will graduate)? ____________
- What percent of classes are taught by professors vs. teaching assistants? ____________
- What is the average class size (Student : Teacher ratio)? ____________________
- What is the expected size of the freshman class? ________________________
- When is the application deadline (regular and early decision)? ____
- When do I need to declare my major and how easy is it to change? ________________
- Do I need to write a thesis to graduate? ________________________________
- Do you take transfer credits? ____________________________________
- What learning opportunities are there outside of the classroom (i.e. internships, coop, research programs)? ____
- How many students typically study abroad? ____________________________
- Are there fraternities and sororities, and what percent of the students belong to one? _______
- What are the popular extracurricular activities? __________________________
- Is there employment placement assistance for graduating seniors? ________________
- What is the cost for tuition? Room and Board? Books and supplies? _______________
- Is there Financial Aid and/or Scholarships available? How do I apply? ______________
- Can freshman live off campus? Can they have a car on campus? _________________
- Do most students stay on campus over weekends or leave? ____________________
- Other questions I have: ______________________________________
- NOTES:

____

____

____

____

____

____

WHAT I LEARNED ABOUT THIS COLLEGE (Page 4 of 6)

Name of College:____

Majors Offered:____

Places I visited during my tour and what I thought of them
Check all that apply and rank from 1 [bad] to 5 [excellent]:

☐ Student Center (-1 2 3 4 5+) comment:______________________________

☐ Computer Center (-1 2 3 4 5+) comment:______________________________

☐ Labs (-1 2 3 4 5+) comment:____________________________________

☐ Lecture Halls (-1 2 3 4 5+) comment:______________________________

☐ Classrooms (-1 2 3 4 5+) comment:________________________________

☐ Department Bldg for my major (-1 2 3 4 5+) comment:____________________

☐ Dormitories (-1 2 3 4 5+) comment:________________________________

☐ Athletic Center / Gym (-1 2 3 4 5+) comment:__________________________

☐ Library (-1 2 3 4 5+) comment:__________________________________

☐ School Store (-1 2 3 4 5+) comment:_______________________________

☐ Dining Hall (-1 2 3 4 5+) comment:________________________________

☐ Other____________________ (-1 2 3 4 5+) comment:____________________

☐ Other____________________ (-1 2 3 4 5+) comment:____________________

☐ Other____________________ (-1 2 3 4 5+) comment:____________________

How was the food?____

What did I think about the campus and the surrounding area:____________________

____

What did I think about the students and the staff I met? Would I fit in well here? ________________

____

What did I think about the courses of study offered here? Do these meet my goals?____________

____

What did I think about the extracurricular activities offered here? ____________________

OVERALL ASSESSMENT and FOLLOW UP ACTIONS (Page 5 of 6)

Name of College:____

What I like best about this college is:______________________________

What I like least about this college is:______________________________

Follow up actions / next steps I need to do are:__________________________

My overall assessment: (-1 2 3 4 5+) comment:____________________

My Parents' overall assessment: (-1 2 3 4 5+) comment:________________

Additional Notes:

Name of College:____

Page 6 of 6 - STAPLE / ATTACH ANY HANDOUTS, MAPS, ETC HERE:

— —

BEFORE YOU GO (Page 1 of 6)

Name of College:____

Location (Street Address):__________________________________

Website URL:____________________ Phone #:____________________

Type of Visit: ☐ Online (Virtual) / ☐ On Site (Tour) Date of Planned On Site Visit:__________

Size of College: ☐ Small (less than 5,000 students) / ☐ Medium (5,000 to 15,000 students) /
☐ Large (more than 15,000 students)

Type of College: ☐ Liberal Arts / ☐ Science & Engineering / ☐ General Studies
☐ College (Undergraduate only) / ☐ University (Undergraduate & Graduate)
☐ State/Community College / ☐ Private College
☐ 2 Year Undergraduate / ☐ 4 Year Undergraduate

Dates / Times of Tours and Information Sessions:__________________________________

Do I know people who are / will be attending this college? ☐ No / ☐ Yes – Name(s):__________

____

Do I know people who have graduated from this college? ☐ No / ☐ Yes – Name(s):__________

____

I am interested in this college because:______________________________

____

Things I have heard about this college are:____________________________

____

WHEN YOU GET THERE (Page 2 of 6)

Name of College:____

Date of Visit:____________________ Time of Visit:____________________

Was school in session when I visited: ☐ Yes / ☐ No

Activities during On Site Visit (check all that apply):

☐ Campus Tour / ☐ Information Session / ☐ Interview / ☐ Tour of Surrounding Area

Surrounding Area: ☐ Rural (Country) / ☐ Suburban (Near residential area) / ☐ Urban (City)

Names of people who presented / people I met with and contact information (phone, email).

____

____

____

Topics discussed at Information Session / notes (see next page for list of possible questions to ask):

____

____

____

____

____

____

____

____

____

____

____

____

WHILE YOU ARE THERE (Page 3 of 6)

Name of College:______________________________

Questions you can ask (some ideas – feel free to modify these or add more):

- What are entrance requirements (GPA, SAT, SAT2, ACT, AP courses, Honors Courses)?
- What is the graduation rate (% of incoming freshmen who will graduate)?
- What percent of classes are taught by professors vs. teaching assistants?
- What is the average class size (Student : Teacher ratio)?
- What is the expected size of the freshman class?
- When is the application deadline (regular and early decision)?
- When do I need to declare my major and how easy is it to change?
- Do I need to write a thesis to graduate?
- Do you take transfer credits?
- What learning opportunities are there outside of the classroom (i.e. internships, coop, research programs)?
- How many students typically study abroad?
- Are there fraternities and sororities, and what percent of the students belong to one?
- What are the popular extracurricular activities?
- Is there employment placement assistance for graduating seniors?
- What is the cost for tuition? Room and Board? Books and supplies?
- Is there Financial Aid and/or Scholarships available? How do I apply?
- Can freshman live off campus? Can they have a car on campus?
- Do most students stay on campus over weekends or leave?
- Other questions I have:
- NOTES:

WHAT I LEARNED ABOUT THIS COLLEGE (Page 4 of 6)

Name of College:____

Majors Offered:____

Places I visited during my tour and what I thought of them
Check all that apply and rank from 1 [bad] to 5 [excellent]:

- ☐ Student Center (-1 2 3 4 5+) comment:____________________________________
- ☐ Computer Center (-1 2 3 4 5+) comment:__________________________________
- ☐ Labs (-1 2 3 4 5+) comment:____
- ☐ Lecture Halls (-1 2 3 4 5+) comment:______________________________________
- ☐ Classrooms (-1 2 3 4 5+) comment:____
- ☐ Department Bldg for my major (-1 2 3 4 5+) comment:___________________________
- ☐ Dormitories (-1 2 3 4 5+) comment:____
- ☐ Athletic Center / Gym (-1 2 3 4 5+) comment:_________________________________
- ☐ Library (-1 2 3 4 5+) comment:____
- ☐ School Store (-1 2 3 4 5+) comment:_______________________________________
- ☐ Dining Hall (-1 2 3 4 5+) comment:_______________________________________
- ☐ Other______________________ (-1 2 3 4 5+) comment:___________________________
- ☐ Other______________________ (-1 2 3 4 5+) comment:___________________________
- ☐ Other______________________ (-1 2 3 4 5+) comment:___________________________

How was the food?____

What did I think about the campus and the surrounding area:________________________________

____

What did I think about the students and the staff I met? Would I fit in well here? ________________

____

What did I think about the courses of study offered here? Do these meet my goals?______________

____

What did I think about the extracurricular activities offered here? __________________________

OVERALL ASSESSMENT and FOLLOW UP ACTIONS (Page 5 of 6)

Name of College:____

What I like best about this college is:______________________________

What I like least about this college is:______________________________

Follow up actions / next steps I need to do are:__________________________

My overall assessment: (-1 2 3 4 5+) comment:____________________

My Parents' overall assessment: (-1 2 3 4 5+) comment:________________

Additional Notes:

Name of College:____

Page 6 of 6 - STAPLE / ATTACH ANY HANDOUTS, MAPS, ETC HERE:

— —

BEFORE YOU GO (Page 1 of 6)

Name of College:____

Location (Street Address):____

Website URL:________________________ Phone #:________________________

Type of Visit: ☐ Online (Virtual) / ☐ On Site (Tour) Date of Planned On Site Visit:__________

Size of College: ☐ Small (less than 5,000 students) / ☐ Medium (5,000 to 15,000 students) /
☐ Large (more than 15,000 students)

Type of College: ☐ Liberal Arts / ☐ Science & Engineering / ☐ General Studies
☐ College (Undergraduate only) / ☐ University (Undergraduate & Graduate)
☐ State/Community College / ☐ Private College
☐ 2 Year Undergraduate / ☐ 4 Year Undergraduate

Dates / Times of Tours and Information Sessions:____________________________________

Do I know people who are / will be attending this college? ☐ No / ☐ Yes – Name(s):__________

____

Do I know people who have graduated from this college? ☐ No / ☐ Yes – Name(s):__________

____

I am interested in this college because:__________________________________

____

Things I have heard about this college are:________________________________

____

WHEN YOU GET THERE (Page 2 of 6)

Name of College:____

Date of Visit:____________________ Time of Visit:____________________

Was school in session when I visited: ☐ Yes / ☐ No

Activities during On Site Visit (check all that apply):

☐ Campus Tour / ☐ Information Session / ☐ Interview / ☐ Tour of Surrounding Area

Surrounding Area: ☐ Rural (Country) / ☐ Suburban (Near residential area) / ☐ Urban (City)

Names of people who presented / people I met with and contact information (phone, email).

____

____

____

Topics discussed at Information Session / notes (see next page for list of possible questions to ask):

____

____

____

____

____

____

____

____

____

____

____

____

WHILE YOU ARE THERE (Page 3 of 6)

Name of College: ______

Questions you can ask (some ideas – feel free to modify these or add more):

- What are entrance requirements (GPA, SAT, SAT2, ACT, AP courses, Honors Courses)? ______
- What is the graduation rate (% of incoming freshmen who will graduate)? ______
- What percent of classes are taught by professors vs. teaching assistants? ______
- What is the average class size (Student : Teacher ratio)? ______
- What is the expected size of the freshman class? ______
- When is the application deadline (regular and early decision)? ______
- When do I need to declare my major and how easy is it to change? ______
- Do I need to write a thesis to graduate? ______
- Do you take transfer credits? ______
- What learning opportunities are there outside of the classroom (i.e. internships, coop, research programs)? ______
- How many students typically study abroad? ______
- Are there fraternities and sororities, and what percent of the students belong to one? ______
- What are the popular extracurricular activities? ______
- Is there employment placement assistance for graduating seniors? ______
- What is the cost for tuition? Room and Board? Books and supplies? ______
- Is there Financial Aid and/or Scholarships available? How do I apply? ______
- Can freshman live off campus? Can they have a car on campus? ______
- Do most students stay on campus over weekends or leave? ______
- Other questions I have: ______
- NOTES:

WHAT I LEARNED ABOUT THIS COLLEGE (Page 4 of 6)

Name of College:____

Majors Offered:____

Places I visited during my tour and what I thought of them
Check all that apply and rank from 1 [bad] to 5 [excellent]:

☐ Student Center (-1 2 3 4 5+) comment:________________________

☐ Computer Center (-1 2 3 4 5+) comment:________________________

☐ Labs (-1 2 3 4 5+) comment:________________________

☐ Lecture Halls (-1 2 3 4 5+) comment:________________________

☐ Classrooms (-1 2 3 4 5+) comment:________________________

☐ Department Bldg for my major (-1 2 3 4 5+) comment:________________________

☐ Dormitories (-1 2 3 4 5+) comment:________________________

☐ Athletic Center / Gym (-1 2 3 4 5+) comment:________________________

☐ Library (-1 2 3 4 5+) comment:________________________

☐ School Store (-1 2 3 4 5+) comment:________________________

☐ Dining Hall (-1 2 3 4 5+) comment:________________________

☐ Other________________ (-1 2 3 4 5+) comment:________________________

☐ Other________________ (-1 2 3 4 5+) comment:________________________

☐ Other________________ (-1 2 3 4 5+) comment:________________________

How was the food?____

What did I think about the campus and the surrounding area:____________________

____

What did I think about the students and the staff I met? Would I fit in well here? ____________

____

What did I think about the courses of study offered here? Do these meet my goals?____________

____

What did I think about the extracurricular activities offered here? ____________________

OVERALL ASSESSMENT and FOLLOW UP ACTIONS (Page 5 of 6)

Name of College:____

What I like best about this college is:______________________________

What I like least about this college is:______________________________

Follow up actions / next steps I need to do are:__________________________

My overall assessment: (-1 2 3 4 5+) comment:____________________

My Parents' overall assessment: (-1 2 3 4 5+) comment:________________

Additional Notes:

Name of College:____

Page 6 of 6 - STAPLE / ATTACH ANY HANDOUTS, MAPS, ETC HERE:

— —

BEFORE YOU GO (Page 1 of 6)

Name of College:____

Location (Street Address):____

Website URL:________________________ Phone #:________________________

Type of Visit: ☐ Online (Virtual) / ☐ On Site (Tour) Date of Planned On Site Visit:____________

Size of College: ☐ Small (less than 5,000 students) / ☐ Medium (5,000 to 15,000 students) /
☐ Large (more than 15,000 students)

Type of College: ☐ Liberal Arts / ☐ Science & Engineering / ☐ General Studies
☐ College (Undergraduate only) / ☐ University (Undergraduate & Graduate)
☐ State/Community College / ☐ Private College
☐ 2 Year Undergraduate / ☐ 4 Year Undergraduate

Dates / Times of Tours and Information Sessions:____

Do I know people who are / will be attending this college? ☐ No / ☐ Yes – Name(s):__________

____

Do I know people who have graduated from this college? ☐ No / ☐ Yes – Name(s):__________

____

I am interested in this college because:____________________________________

____

Things I have heard about this college are:__________________________________

____

WHEN YOU GET THERE (Page 2 of 6)

Name of College:____

Date of Visit:____________________ Time of Visit:____________________

Was school in session when I visited: ☐ Yes / ☐ No

Activities during On Site Visit (check all that apply):

☐ Campus Tour / ☐ Information Session / ☐ Interview / ☐ Tour of Surrounding Area

Surrounding Area: ☐ Rural (Country) / ☐ Suburban (Near residential area) / ☐ Urban (City)

Names of people who presented / people I met with and contact information (phone, email).

____

____

____

Topics discussed at Information Session / notes (see next page for list of possible questions to ask):

____

____

____

____

____

____

____

____

____

____

____

____

WHILE YOU ARE THERE (Page 3 of 6)

Namc of College:____

Questions you can ask (some ideas – feel free to modify these or add more):

- What are entrance requirements (GPA, SAT, SAT2, ACT, AP courses, Honors Courses)? ________________________
- What is the graduation rate (% of incoming freshmen who will graduate)? __________
- What percent of classes are taught by professors vs. teaching assistants? __________
- What is the average class size (Student : Teacher ratio)? __________
- What is the expected size of the freshman class? __________
- When is the application deadline (regular and early decision)? ________________________
- When do I need to declare my major and how easy is it to change? __________
- Do I need to write a thesis to graduate? __________
- Do you take transfer credits? __________
- What learning opportunities are there outside of the classroom (i.e. internships, coop, research programs)? __________
- How many students typically study abroad? __________
- Are there fraternities and sororities, and what percent of the students belong to one? __________
- What are the popular extracurricular activities? __________
- Is there employment placement assistance for graduating seniors? __________
- What is the cost for tuition? Room and Board? Books and supplies? __________
- Is there Financial Aid and/or Scholarships available? How do I apply? __________
- Can freshman live off campus? Can they have a car on campus? __________
- Do most students stay on campus over weekends or leave? __________
- Other questions I have: __________
- NOTES:

____

____

____

____

____

____

WHAT I LEARNED ABOUT THIS COLLEGE (Page 4 of 6)

Name of College:____

Majors Offered:____

Places I visited during my tour and what I thought of them
Check all that apply and rank from 1 [bad] to 5 [excellent]:

☐ Student Center (-1 2 3 4 5+) comment:____________________

☐ Computer Center (-1 2 3 4 5+) comment:____________________

☐ Labs (-1 2 3 4 5+) comment:____________________

☐ Lecture Halls (-1 2 3 4 5+) comment:____________________

☐ Classrooms (-1 2 3 4 5+) comment:____________________

☐ Department Bldg for my major (-1 2 3 4 5+) comment:____________________

☐ Dormitories (-1 2 3 4 5+) comment:____________________

☐ Athletic Center / Gym (-1 2 3 4 5+) comment:____________________

☐ Library (-1 2 3 4 5+) comment:____________________

☐ School Store (-1 2 3 4 5+) comment:____________________

☐ Dining Hall (-1 2 3 4 5+) comment:____________________

☐ Other________________ (-1 2 3 4 5+) comment:____________________

☐ Other________________ (-1 2 3 4 5+) comment:____________________

☐ Other________________ (-1 2 3 4 5+) comment:____________________

How was the food?____

What did I think about the campus and the surrounding area:____________________

____

What did I think about the students and the staff I met? Would I fit in well here? ________________

____

What did I think about the courses of study offered here? Do these meet my goals?________________

____

What did I think about the extracurricular activities offered here? ____________________

OVERALL ASSESSMENT and FOLLOW UP ACTIONS (Page 5 of 6)

Name of College:____

What I like best about this college is:______________________________

What I like least about this college is:______________________________

Follow up actions / next steps I need to do are:__________________________

My overall assessment: (-1 2 3 4 5+) comment:____________________

My Parents' overall assessment: (-1 2 3 4 5+) comment:________________

Additional Notes:

Name of College:____

Page 6 of 6 - STAPLE / ATTACH ANY HANDOUTS, MAPS, ETC HERE:

— —

BEFORE YOU GO (Page 1 of 6)

Name of College:____

Location (Street Address):____

Website URL:________________________ Phone #:________________________

Type of Visit: ☐ Online (Virtual) / ☐ On Site (Tour) Date of Planned On Site Visit:__________

Size of College: ☐ Small (less than 5,000 students) / ☐ Medium (5,000 to 15,000 students) /
☐ Large (more than 15,000 students)

Type of College: ☐ Liberal Arts / ☐ Science & Engineering / ☐ General Studies
☐ College (Undergraduate only) / ☐ University (Undergraduate & Graduate)
☐ State/Community College / ☐ Private College
☐ 2 Year Undergraduate / ☐ 4 Year Undergraduate

Dates / Times of Tours and Information Sessions:____

Do I know people who are / will be attending this college? ☐ No / ☐ Yes – Name(s):__________

____

Do I know people who have graduated from this college? ☐ No / ☐ Yes – Name(s):__________

____

I am interested in this college because:____

____

Things I have heard about this college are:______________________________________

____

WHEN YOU GET THERE (Page 2 of 6)

Name of College:____

Date of Visit:____________________ Time of Visit:____________________

Was school in session when I visited: ☐ Yes / ☐ No

Activities during On Site Visit (check all that apply):

☐ Campus Tour / ☐ Information Session / ☐ Interview / ☐ Tour of Surrounding Area

Surrounding Area: ☐ Rural (Country) / ☐ Suburban (Near residential area) / ☐ Urban (City)

Names of people who presented / people I met with and contact information (phone, email).

____

____

____

Topics discussed at Information Session / notes (see next page for list of possible questions to ask):

____

____

____

____

____

____

____

____

____

____

____

____

WHILE YOU ARE THERE (Page 3 of 6)

Name of College: ______________________________

Questions you can ask (some ideas – feel free to modify these or add more):

- What are entrance requirements (GPA, SAT, SAT2, ACT, AP courses, Honors Courses)? ______________________________
- What is the graduation rate (% of incoming freshmen who will graduate)? ______________
- What percent of classes are taught by professors vs. teaching assistants? ______________
- What is the average class size (Student : Teacher ratio)? ______________
- What is the expected size of the freshman class? ______________
- When is the application deadline (regular and early decision)? ______________________________
- When do I need to declare my major and how easy is it to change? ______________
- Do I need to write a thesis to graduate? ______________
- Do you take transfer credits? ______________
- What learning opportunities are there outside of the classroom (i.e. internships, coop, research programs)? ______________
- How many students typically study abroad? ______________
- Are there fraternities and sororities, and what percent of the students belong to one? ______________
- What are the popular extracurricular activities? ______________
- Is there employment placement assistance for graduating seniors? ______________
- What is the cost for tuition? Room and Board? Books and supplies? ______________
- Is there Financial Aid and/or Scholarships available? How do I apply? ______________
- Can freshman live off campus? Can they have a car on campus? ______________
- Do most students stay on campus over weekends or leave? ______________
- Other questions I have: ______________
- NOTES:

____

____

____

____

____

____

WHAT I LEARNED ABOUT THIS COLLEGE (Page 4 of 6)

Name of College:______________________________

Majors Offered:______________________________

Places I visited during my tour and what I thought of them
Check all that apply and rank from 1 [bad] to 5 [excellent]:

☐ Student Center (-1 2 3 4 5+) comment:______________

☐ Computer Center (-1 2 3 4 5+) comment:______________

☐ Labs (-1 2 3 4 5+) comment:______________

☐ Lecture Halls (-1 2 3 4 5+) comment:______________

☐ Classrooms (-1 2 3 4 5+) comment:______________

☐ Department Bldg for my major (-1 2 3 4 5+) comment:______________

☐ Dormitories (-1 2 3 4 5+) comment:______________

☐ Athletic Center / Gym (-1 2 3 4 5+) comment:______________

☐ Library (-1 2 3 4 5+) comment:______________

☐ School Store (-1 2 3 4 5+) comment:______________

☐ Dining Hall (-1 2 3 4 5+) comment:______________

☐ Other______________ (-1 2 3 4 5+) comment:______________

☐ Other______________ (-1 2 3 4 5+) comment:______________

☐ Other______________ (-1 2 3 4 5+) comment:______________

How was the food?______________________________

What did I think about the campus and the surrounding area:______________

____

What did I think about the students and the staff I met? Would I fit in well here? ______________

____

What did I think about the courses of study offered here? Do these meet my goals?______________

____

What did I think about the extracurricular activities offered here? ______________

OVERALL ASSESSMENT and FOLLOW UP ACTIONS (Page 5 of 6)

Name of College:____

What I like best about this college is:______________________________

What I like least about this college is:______________________________

Follow up actions / next steps I need to do are:__________________________

My overall assessment: (-1 2 3 4 5+) comment:____________________

My Parents' overall assessment: (-1 2 3 4 5+) comment:________________

Additional Notes:

Name of College:____

Page 6 of 6 - STAPLE / ATTACH ANY HANDOUTS, MAPS, ETC HERE:

— —

BEFORE YOU GO (Page 1 of 6)

Name of College:____

Location (Street Address):_______________________________________

Website URL:_________________________ Phone #:_________________________

Type of Visit: ☐ Online (Virtual) / ☐ On Site (Tour) Date of Planned On Site Visit:__________

Size of College: ☐ Small (less than 5,000 students) / ☐ Medium (5,000 to 15,000 students) /
☐ Large (more than 15,000 students)

Type of College: ☐ Liberal Arts / ☐ Science & Engineering / ☐ General Studies
☐ College (Undergraduate only) / ☐ University (Undergraduate & Graduate)
☐ State/Community College / ☐ Private College
☐ 2 Year Undergraduate / ☐ 4 Year Undergraduate

Dates / Times of Tours and Information Sessions:____

Do I know people who are / will be attending this college? ☐ No / ☐ Yes – Name(s):__________

____

Do I know people who have graduated from this college? ☐ No / ☐ Yes – Name(s):__________

____

I am interested in this college because:______________________________

____

Things I have heard about this college are:____________________________

____

WHEN YOU GET THERE (Page 2 of 6)

Name of College:____

Date of Visit:____________________ Time of Visit:____________________

Was school in session when I visited: ☐ Yes / ☐ No

Activities during On Site Visit (check all that apply):

☐ Campus Tour / ☐ Information Session / ☐ Interview / ☐ Tour of Surrounding Area

Surrounding Area: ☐ Rural (Country) / ☐ Suburban (Near residential area) / ☐ Urban (City)

Names of people who presented / people I met with and contact information (phone, email).

____

____

____

Topics discussed at Information Session / notes (see next page for list of possible questions to ask):

____

____

____

____

____

____

____

____

____

____

____

____

WHILE YOU ARE THERE (Page 3 of 6)

Name of College:____

Questions you can ask (some ideas – feel free to modify these or add more):

- What are entrance requirements (GPA, SAT, SAT2, ACT, AP courses, Honors Courses)? ____
- What is the graduation rate (% of incoming freshmen who will graduate)? ________________
- What percent of classes are taught by professors vs. teaching assistants? ________________
- What is the average class size (Student : Teacher ratio)? __________________________
- What is the expected size of the freshman class? ________________________________
- When is the application deadline (regular and early decision)? ____
- When do I need to declare my major and how easy is it to change? ____________________
- Do I need to write a thesis to graduate? ____
- Do you take transfer credits? ____
- What learning opportunities are there outside of the classroom (i.e. internships, coop, research programs)? ____
- How many students typically study abroad? _____________________________________
- Are there fraternities and sororities, and what percent of the students belong to one? ________
- What are the popular extracurricular activities? __________________________________
- Is there employment placement assistance for graduating seniors? ____________________
- What is the cost for tuition? Room and Board? Books and supplies? __________________
- Is there Financial Aid and/or Scholarships available? How do I apply? _________________
- Can freshman live off campus? Can they have a car on campus? _____________________
- Do most students stay on campus over weekends or leave? _________________________
- Other questions I have: ____
- NOTES:

____

____

____

____

____

____

WHAT I LEARNED ABOUT THIS COLLEGE (Page 4 of 6)

Name of College:____

Majors Offered:____

Places I visited during my tour and what I thought of them
Check all that apply and rank from 1 [bad] to 5 [excellent]:

☐ Student Center (-1 2 3 4 5+) comment:______________________________

☐ Computer Center (-1 2 3 4 5+) comment:______________________________

☐ Labs (-1 2 3 4 5+) comment:__________________________________

☐ Lecture Halls (-1 2 3 4 5+) comment:______________________________

☐ Classrooms (-1 2 3 4 5+) comment:_______________________________

☐ Department Bldg for my major (-1 2 3 4 5+) comment:____________________

☐ Dormitories (-1 2 3 4 5+) comment:_______________________________

☐ Athletic Center / Gym (-1 2 3 4 5+) comment:_________________________

☐ Library (-1 2 3 4 5+) comment:_________________________________

☐ School Store (-1 2 3 4 5+) comment:______________________________

☐ Dining Hall (-1 2 3 4 5+) comment:_______________________________

☐ Other__________________ (-1 2 3 4 5+) comment:____________________

☐ Other__________________ (-1 2 3 4 5+) comment:____________________

☐ Other__________________ (-1 2 3 4 5+) comment:____________________

How was the food?____

What did I think about the campus and the surrounding area:____________________

____

What did I think about the students and the staff I met? Would I fit in well here? __________

____

What did I think about the courses of study offered here? Do these meet my goals?__________

____

What did I think about the extracurricular activities offered here? __________________

OVERALL ASSESSMENT and FOLLOW UP ACTIONS (Page 5 of 6)

Name of College:____

What I like best about this college is:______________________________

____

____

____

What I like least about this college is:______________________________

____

____

____

Follow up actions / next steps I need to do are:_______________________

____

____

____

My overall assessment: (-1 2 3 4 5+) comment:____________________

My Parents' overall assessment: (-1 2 3 4 5+) comment:______________

Additional Notes:

____

____

____

____

____

____

____

____

____

____

____

____

Name of College:____

Page 6 of 6 - STAPLE / ATTACH ANY HANDOUTS, MAPS, ETC HERE:

— —

BEFORE YOU GO (Page 1 of 6)

Name of College:____

Location (Street Address):____________________________________

Website URL:________________________ Phone #:________________________

Type of Visit: ☐ Online (Virtual) / ☐ On Site (Tour) Date of Planned On Site Visit:__________

Size of College: ☐ Small (less than 5,000 students) / ☐ Medium (5,000 to 15,000 students) /
☐ Large (more than 15,000 students)

Type of College: ☐ Liberal Arts / ☐ Science & Engineering / ☐ General Studies
☐ College (Undergraduate only) / ☐ University (Undergraduate & Graduate)
☐ State/Community College / ☐ Private College
☐ 2 Year Undergraduate / ☐ 4 Year Undergraduate

Dates / Times of Tours and Information
Sessions:____

Do I know people who are / will be attending this college? ☐ No / ☐ Yes – Name(s):__________

____

Do I know people who have graduated from this college? ☐ No / ☐ Yes – Name(s):__________

____

I am interested in this college because:______________________________

____

Things I have heard about this college are:____________________________

____

WHEN YOU GET THERE (Page 2 of 6)

Name of College:____

Date of Visit:________________________ Time of Visit:________________________

Was school in session when I visited: ☐ Yes / ☐ No

Activities during On Site Visit (check all that apply):

☐ Campus Tour / ☐ Information Session / ☐ Interview / ☐ Tour of Surrounding Area

Surrounding Area: ☐ Rural (Country) / ☐ Suburban (Near residential area) / ☐ Urban (City)

Names of people who presented / people I met with and contact information (phone, email).

____

____

____

Topics discussed at Information Session / notes (see next page for list of possible questions to ask):

____

____

____

____

____

____

____

____

____

____

____

____

WHILE YOU ARE THERE (Page 3 of 6)

Name of College:______________________________

Questions you can ask (some ideas – feel free to modify these or add more):

- What are entrance requirements (GPA, SAT, SAT2, ACT, AP courses, Honors Courses)? ______________________________
- What is the graduation rate (% of incoming freshmen who will graduate)? ______________
- What percent of classes are taught by professors vs. teaching assistants? ______________
- What is the average class size (Student : Teacher ratio)? ______________
- What is the expected size of the freshman class? ______________
- When is the application deadline (regular and early decision)? ______________________________
- When do I need to declare my major and how easy is it to change? ______________
- Do I need to write a thesis to graduate? ______________
- Do you take transfer credits? ______________
- What learning opportunities are there outside of the classroom (i.e. internships, coop, research programs)? ______________
- How many students typically study abroad? ______________
- Are there fraternities and sororities, and what percent of the students belong to one? ________
- What are the popular extracurricular activities? ______________
- Is there employment placement assistance for graduating seniors? ______________
- What is the cost for tuition? Room and Board? Books and supplies? ______________
- Is there Financial Aid and/or Scholarships available? How do I apply? ______________
- Can freshman live off campus? Can they have a car on campus? ______________
- Do most students stay on campus over weekends or leave? ______________
- Other questions I have: ______________
- NOTES:

____

____

____

____

____

____

WHAT I LEARNED ABOUT THIS COLLEGE (Page 4 of 6)

Name of College:____

Majors Offered:____

Places I visited during my tour and what I thought of them
Check all that apply and rank from 1 [bad] to 5 [excellent]:

☐ Student Center (-1 2 3 4 5+) comment:____________________

☐ Computer Center (-1 2 3 4 5+) comment:____________________

☐ Labs (-1 2 3 4 5+) comment:____________________

☐ Lecture Halls (-1 2 3 4 5+) comment:____________________

☐ Classrooms (-1 2 3 4 5+) comment:____________________

☐ Department Bldg for my major (-1 2 3 4 5+) comment:____________________

☐ Dormitories (-1 2 3 4 5+) comment:____________________

☐ Athletic Center / Gym (-1 2 3 4 5+) comment:____________________

☐ Library (-1 2 3 4 5+) comment:____________________

☐ School Store (-1 2 3 4 5+) comment:____________________

☐ Dining Hall (-1 2 3 4 5+) comment:____________________

☐ Other________________ (-1 2 3 4 5+) comment:____________________

☐ Other________________ (-1 2 3 4 5+) comment:____________________

☐ Other________________ (-1 2 3 4 5+) comment:____________________

How was the food?____

What did I think about the campus and the surrounding area:____________________

____

What did I think about the students and the staff I met? Would I fit in well here? ________________

____

What did I think about the courses of study offered here? Do these meet my goals?________________

____

What did I think about the extracurricular activities offered here? ____________________

OVERALL ASSESSMENT and FOLLOW UP ACTIONS (Page 5 of 6)

Name of College:____

What I like best about this college is:________________________________

What I like least about this college is:_______________________________

Follow up actions / next steps I need to do are:__________________________

My overall assessment: (-1 2 3 4 5+) comment:______________________

My Parents' overall assessment: (-1 2 3 4 5+) comment:__________________

Additional Notes:

Name of College:____

Page 6 of 6 - STAPLE / ATTACH ANY HANDOUTS, MAPS, ETC HERE:

— —

BEFORE YOU GO (Page 1 of 6)

Name of College:____

Location (Street Address):____

Website URL:____________________________ Phone #:____________________________

Type of Visit: ☐ Online (Virtual) / ☐ On Site (Tour) Date of Planned On Site Visit:____________

Size of College: ☐ Small (less than 5,000 students) / ☐ Medium (5,000 to 15,000 students) /
☐ Large (more than 15,000 students)

Type of College: ☐ Liberal Arts / ☐ Science & Engineering / ☐ General Studies
☐ College (Undergraduate only) / ☐ University (Undergraduate & Graduate)
☐ State/Community College / ☐ Private College
☐ 2 Year Undergraduate / ☐ 4 Year Undergraduate

Dates / Times of Tours and Information
Sessions:____

Do I know people who are / will be attending this college? ☐ No / ☐ Yes – Name(s):____________

____

Do I know people who have graduated from this college? ☐ No / ☐ Yes – Name(s):____________

____

I am interested in this college because:____

____

Things I have heard about this college are:_______________________________________

____

WHEN YOU GET THERE (Page 2 of 6)

Name of College:____

Date of Visit:____________________ Time of Visit:____________________

Was school in session when I visited: ☐ Yes / ☐ No

Activities during On Site Visit (check all that apply):

☐ Campus Tour / ☐ Information Session / ☐ Interview / ☐ Tour of Surrounding Area

Surrounding Area: ☐ Rural (Country) / ☐ Suburban (Near residential area) / ☐ Urban (City)

Names of people who presented / people I met with and contact information (phone, email).

Topics discussed at Information Session / notes (see next page for list of possible questions to ask):

WHILE YOU ARE THERE (Page 3 of 6)

Name of College: ______________________________

Questions you can ask (some ideas – feel free to modify these or add more):

- What are entrance requirements (GPA, SAT, SAT2, ACT, AP courses, Honors Courses)? ______________________________
- What is the graduation rate (% of incoming freshmen who will graduate)? ______________
- What percent of classes are taught by professors vs. teaching assistants? ______________
- What is the average class size (Student : Teacher ratio)? ______________
- What is the expected size of the freshman class? ______________
- When is the application deadline (regular and early decision)? ______________________________
- When do I need to declare my major and how easy is it to change? ______________
- Do I need to write a thesis to graduate? ______________
- Do you take transfer credits? ______________
- What learning opportunities are there outside of the classroom (i.e. internships, coop, research programs)? ______________
- How many students typically study abroad? ______________
- Are there fraternities and sororities, and what percent of the students belong to one? ________
- What are the popular extracurricular activities? ______________
- Is there employment placement assistance for graduating seniors? ______________
- What is the cost for tuition? Room and Board? Books and supplies? ______________
- Is there Financial Aid and/or Scholarships available? How do I apply? ______________
- Can freshman live off campus? Can they have a car on campus? ______________
- Do most students stay on campus over weekends or leave? ______________
- Other questions I have: ______________
- NOTES:

____

____

____

____

____

____

WHAT I LEARNED ABOUT THIS COLLEGE (Page 4 of 6)

Name of College:______________________________

Majors Offered:______________________________

Places I visited during my tour and what I thought of them
Check all that apply and rank from 1 [bad] to 5 [excellent]:

☐ Student Center (-1 2 3 4 5+) comment:________________

☐ Computer Center (-1 2 3 4 5+) comment:________________

☐ Labs (-1 2 3 4 5+) comment:________________

☐ Lecture Halls (-1 2 3 4 5+) comment:________________

☐ Classrooms (-1 2 3 4 5+) comment:________________

☐ Department Bldg for my major (-1 2 3 4 5+) comment:________________

☐ Dormitories (-1 2 3 4 5+) comment:________________

☐ Athletic Center / Gym (-1 2 3 4 5+) comment:________________

☐ Library (-1 2 3 4 5+) comment:________________

☐ School Store (-1 2 3 4 5+) comment:________________

☐ Dining Hall (-1 2 3 4 5+) comment:________________

☐ Other____________ (-1 2 3 4 5+) comment:________________

☐ Other____________ (-1 2 3 4 5+) comment:________________

☐ Other____________ (-1 2 3 4 5+) comment:________________

How was the food?______________________________

What did I think about the campus and the surrounding area:________________

____

What did I think about the students and the staff I met? Would I fit in well here? ____________

____

What did I think about the courses of study offered here? Do these meet my goals?____________

____

What did I think about the extracurricular activities offered here? ________________

OVERALL ASSESSMENT and FOLLOW UP ACTIONS (Page 5 of 6)

Name of College:____

What I like best about this college is:______________________________

What I like least about this college is:______________________________

Follow up actions / next steps I need to do are:__________________________

My overall assessment: (-1 2 3 4 5+) comment:______________________

My Parents' overall assessment: (-1 2 3 4 5+) comment:__________________

Additional Notes:

Name of College:____

Page 6 of 6 - STAPLE / ATTACH ANY HANDOUTS, MAPS, ETC HERE:

— —

BEFORE YOU GO (Page 1 of 6)

Name of College:____

Location (Street Address):____

Website URL:________________________ Phone #:________________________

Type of Visit: ☐ Online (Virtual) / ☐ On Site (Tour) Date of Planned On Site Visit:__________

Size of College: ☐ Small (less than 5,000 students) / ☐ Medium (5,000 to 15,000 students) /
☐ Large (more than 15,000 students)

Type of College: ☐ Liberal Arts / ☐ Science & Engineering / ☐ General Studies
☐ College (Undergraduate only) / ☐ University (Undergraduate & Graduate)
☐ State/Community College / ☐ Private College
☐ 2 Year Undergraduate / ☐ 4 Year Undergraduate

Dates / Times of Tours and Information Sessions:____

Do I know people who are / will be attending this college? ☐ No / ☐ Yes – Name(s):__________

____

Do I know people who have graduated from this college? ☐ No / ☐ Yes – Name(s):__________

____

I am interested in this college because:____________________________________

____

Things I have heard about this college are:_________________________________

____

WHEN YOU GET THERE (Page 2 of 6)

Name of College:____

Date of Visit:______________________ Time of Visit:______________________

Was school in session when I visited: ☐ Yes / ☐ No

Activities during On Site Visit (check all that apply):

☐ Campus Tour / ☐ Information Session / ☐ Interview / ☐ Tour of Surrounding Area

Surrounding Area: ☐ Rural (Country) / ☐ Suburban (Near residential area) / ☐ Urban (City)

Names of people who presented / people I met with and contact information (phone, email).

____

____

____

Topics discussed at Information Session / notes (see next page for list of possible questions to ask):

____

____

____

____

____

____

____

____

____

____

____

____

WHILE YOU ARE THERE (Page 3 of 6)

Name of College: ______________________________

Questions you can ask (some ideas – feel free to modify these or add more):

- What are entrance requirements (GPA, SAT, SAT2, ACT, AP courses, Honors Courses)? ______________________________
- What is the graduation rate (% of incoming freshmen who will graduate)? ____________
- What percent of classes are taught by professors vs. teaching assistants? ____________
- What is the average class size (Student : Teacher ratio)? ____________
- What is the expected size of the freshman class? ____________
- When is the application deadline (regular and early decision)? ______________________________
- When do I need to declare my major and how easy is it to change? ____________
- Do I need to write a thesis to graduate? ____________
- Do you take transfer credits? ____________
- What learning opportunities are there outside of the classroom (i.e. internships, coop, research programs)? ____________
- How many students typically study abroad? ____________
- Are there fraternities and sororities, and what percent of the students belong to one? ________
- What are the popular extracurricular activities? ____________
- Is there employment placement assistance for graduating seniors? ____________
- What is the cost for tuition? Room and Board? Books and supplies? ____________
- Is there Financial Aid and/or Scholarships available? How do I apply? ____________
- Can freshman live off campus? Can they have a car on campus? ____________
- Do most students stay on campus over weekends or leave? ____________
- Other questions I have: ____________
- NOTES:

____

____

____

____

____

____

WHAT I LEARNED ABOUT THIS COLLEGE (Page 4 of 6)

Name of College:______________________________

Majors Offered:______________________________

Places I visited during my tour and what I thought of them
Check all that apply and rank from 1 [bad] to 5 [excellent]:

☐ Student Center (-1 2 3 4 5+) comment:____________________

☐ Computer Center (-1 2 3 4 5+) comment:____________________

☐ Labs (-1 2 3 4 5+) comment:____________________

☐ Lecture Halls (-1 2 3 4 5+) comment:____________________

☐ Classrooms (-1 2 3 4 5+) comment:____________________

☐ Department Bldg for my major (-1 2 3 4 5+) comment:____________________

☐ Dormitories (-1 2 3 4 5+) comment:____________________

☐ Athletic Center / Gym (-1 2 3 4 5+) comment:____________________

☐ Library (-1 2 3 4 5+) comment:____________________

☐ School Store (-1 2 3 4 5+) comment:____________________

☐ Dining Hall (-1 2 3 4 5+) comment:____________________

☐ Other________________ (-1 2 3 4 5+) comment:____________________

☐ Other________________ (-1 2 3 4 5+) comment:____________________

☐ Other________________ (-1 2 3 4 5+) comment:____________________

How was the food?______________________________

What did I think about the campus and the surrounding area:____________________

____

What did I think about the students and the staff I met? Would I fit in well here? ________________

____

What did I think about the courses of study offered here? Do these meet my goals?________________

____

What did I think about the extracurricular activities offered here? ____________________

OVERALL ASSESSMENT and FOLLOW UP ACTIONS (Page 5 of 6)

Name of College:____

What I like best about this college is:______________________________

What I like least about this college is:______________________________

Follow up actions / next steps I need to do are:______________________________

My overall assessment: (-1 2 3 4 5+) comment:________________________

My Parents' overall assessment: (-1 2 3 4 5+) comment:____________________

Additional Notes:

Name of College:____

Page 6 of 6 - STAPLE / ATTACH ANY HANDOUTS, MAPS, ETC HERE:

— —

BEFORE YOU GO (Page 1 of 6)

Name of College:____

Location (Street Address):______________________________________

Website URL:____________________ Phone #:____________________

Type of Visit: ☐ Online (Virtual) / ☐ On Site (Tour) Date of Planned On Site Visit:__________

Size of College: ☐ Small (less than 5,000 students) / ☐ Medium (5,000 to 15,000 students) /
☐ Large (more than 15,000 students)

Type of College: ☐ Liberal Arts / ☐ Science & Engineering / ☐ General Studies
☐ College (Undergraduate only) / ☐ University (Undergraduate & Graduate)
☐ State/Community College / ☐ Private College
☐ 2 Year Undergraduate / ☐ 4 Year Undergraduate

Dates / Times of Tours and Information Sessions:______________________________________

Do I know people who are / will be attending this college? ☐ No / ☐ Yes – Name(s):__________

____

Do I know people who have graduated from this college? ☐ No / ☐ Yes – Name(s):__________

____

I am interested in this college because:________________________________

____

Things I have heard about this college are:______________________________

____

WHEN YOU GET THERE (Page 2 of 6)

Name of College:____

Date of Visit:________________________ Time of Visit:________________________

Was school in session when I visited: ☐ Yes / ☐ No

Activities during On Site Visit (check all that apply):

☐ Campus Tour / ☐ Information Session / ☐ Interview / ☐ Tour of Surrounding Area

Surrounding Area: ☐ Rural (Country) / ☐ Suburban (Near residential area) / ☐ Urban (City)

Names of people who presented / people I met with and contact information (phone, email).

____

____

____

Topics discussed at Information Session / notes (see next page for list of possible questions to ask):

____

____

____

____

____

____

____

____

____

____

____

____

WHILE YOU ARE THERE (Page 3 of 6)

Name of College:________________________________

Questions you can ask (some ideas – feel free to modify these or add more):

- What are entrance requirements (GPA, SAT, SAT2, ACT, AP courses, Honors Courses)? ____________________
- What is the graduation rate (% of incoming freshmen who will graduate)? __________
- What percent of classes are taught by professors vs. teaching assistants? __________
- What is the average class size (Student : Teacher ratio)? __________
- What is the expected size of the freshman class? __________
- When is the application deadline (regular and early decision)? ____________________
- When do I need to declare my major and how easy is it to change? __________
- Do I need to write a thesis to graduate? __________
- Do you take transfer credits? __________
- What learning opportunities are there outside of the classroom (i.e. internships, coop, research programs)? __________
- How many students typically study abroad? __________
- Are there fraternities and sororities, and what percent of the students belong to one? __________
- What are the popular extracurricular activities? __________
- Is there employment placement assistance for graduating seniors? __________
- What is the cost for tuition? Room and Board? Books and supplies? __________
- Is there Financial Aid and/or Scholarships available? How do I apply? __________
- Can freshman live off campus? Can they have a car on campus? __________
- Do most students stay on campus over weekends or leave? __________
- Other questions I have: __________
- NOTES:

____

____

____

____

____

____

WHAT I LEARNED ABOUT THIS COLLEGE (Page 4 of 6)

Name of College:______________________________

Majors Offered:______________________________

Places I visited during my tour and what I thought of them
Check all that apply and rank from 1 [bad] to 5 [excellent]:

☐ Student Center (-1 2 3 4 5+) comment:____________________

☐ Computer Center (-1 2 3 4 5+) comment:____________________

☐ Labs (-1 2 3 4 5+) comment:____________________

☐ Lecture Halls (-1 2 3 4 5+) comment:____________________

☐ Classrooms (-1 2 3 4 5+) comment:____________________

☐ Department Bldg for my major (-1 2 3 4 5+) comment:____________________

☐ Dormitories (-1 2 3 4 5+) comment:____________________

☐ Athletic Center / Gym (-1 2 3 4 5+) comment:____________________

☐ Library (-1 2 3 4 5+) comment:____________________

☐ School Store (-1 2 3 4 5+) comment:____________________

☐ Dining Hall (-1 2 3 4 5+) comment:____________________

☐ Other________________ (-1 2 3 4 5+) comment:____________________

☐ Other________________ (-1 2 3 4 5+) comment:____________________

☐ Other________________ (-1 2 3 4 5+) comment:____________________

How was the food?______________________________

What did I think about the campus and the surrounding area:____________________

____

What did I think about the students and the staff I met? Would I fit in well here? ____________________

____

What did I think about the courses of study offered here? Do these meet my goals?____________________

____

What did I think about the extracurricular activities offered here? ____________________

OVERALL ASSESSMENT and FOLLOW UP ACTIONS (Page 5 of 6)

Name of College:____

What I like best about this college is:____________________________________

What I like least about this college is:____________________________________

Follow up actions / next steps I need to do are:________________________________

My overall assessment: (-1 2 3 4 5+) comment:__________________________

My Parents' overall assessment: (-1 2 3 4 5+) comment:_____________________

Additional Notes:

Name of College:____

Page 6 of 6 - STAPLE / ATTACH ANY HANDOUTS, MAPS, ETC HERE:

— —

Made in the USA
Middletown, DE
21 May 2018